Getting Out

One Expat's Journey to a New Life in Italy

Cover Photo by Mario Errico: Ponte della Maddalen, Comune di Borgo a Mozzano.

"Getting Out: One Expat's Journey to a New Life in Italy," by Carla Bastos. ISBN 978-1-63868-082-6.

Published 2022 by Virtualbookworm.com Publishing Inc., P.O. Box 9949, College Station, TX 77842, US.

To Zendejas

Contents

Introduction

In late 2021, a friend suggested I gather all of my research and notes in which I'd documented my journey to becoming an expat in Italy, and pull them together into a book. He felt there was a need for such a book because of today's exploding numbers of aspiring expats, particularly from the U.S.

The thought had occurred to me. But, upon reading seemingly endless accounts from other expats, I actually didn't think there was a need for yet another. Then something else occurred to me. Each account was different. Each experience was different, not only because each expat may have had different plans or motivations, or chosen a different country in which to settle, but because they were different *people.*

I realized that, because each experience was unique, each one added something valuable to the big picture. So, perhaps my two cents would, too.

Just one caveat. If you're looking for a comprehensive, how-to manual to guide you on your road to the expat life, you've come to the wrong place. This is not that. Nor is it a feel-good account of blind optimism, or the makings of a Hollywood script. Whatever you may have seen or read may well have been some people's experiences, but those narratives may or may not apply in your life. Even if you are a single, female, Black American retiree who decides to move to Italy, your experience will likely be vastly different than mine.

What I have tried to share in these pages are the requisite *who, what, when, where* and *why* of my own real-world experience, that may serve as a starting point to create yours. (Although admittedly, I've always had a problem with the order of those *W*s. Considering the *why* as a final element in news stories is fine, but when making life-altering decisions it borders on insanity.)

My priorities in preparing for this journey will be discussed in detail because, in my view, thoroughness in the preparation process may be the single most important key. But, because those key factors that were priorities for me may not be for you, I'll encourage lots of self-examination here. I've tried not to be too sappy, but soul searching is an important first step in the process and must not be neglected. I see it more as pragmatism than emotionalism.

Besides the preparation process, I will also discuss here the rigorous requirements and administrative steps along the way, as well as some of the essential elements that helped me adapt once I arrived in Italy. I learned that all the preparation in the world would not have completely equipped me for my new life. There were many things that I just had to learn on the fly or make up as I went. For example, I found that a touch of the familiar at just the right time could make all the difference on any given day—and this journey is most certainly a day-by-day proposition.

From a few comforts of home to learning more about the culture and history of my new country, and activities that provided a bridge to connect the two, I hope to give you some insight into what those first few weeks and months might hold—and how you can make them more of a smooth transition and less of a culture shock. I'll share a few of my favorite things and places and people in my new home country, and perhaps help stir up your own understanding of what draws you to a particular region.

Be prepared for a few surprises. Like most things in life, the journey is not always as rosy as you might think. Several new and aspiring expats I spoke with seemed to have what I call "rose-colored glasses syndrome," so I'll encourage you to lose those specs and join me in the real world. At times it may all be a little daunting, but the new discoveries and learning experiences, both the good and the bad, are part of what makes the whole thing worthwhile.

Kudos to you for having the courage, the curiosity, and that touch of crazy that it takes to pursue what is sure to be the experience of a lifetime. I do hope you'll find takeaways here that will help you on your journey. Because I needed all the help I could get on mine.

* * *

And You Are?

One of the most rewarding decisions I've made in life was the decision to be a lifelong learner. Not that it was even a conscious choice in the beginning. It came almost by accident back in my early 20s when a girlfriend and I, both single parents at the time, decided to move from New Jersey to California. Driving cluelessly across the country in a '69 Camaro was an eye-opener I could never have anticipated.

I'd traveled little up to that point, mostly around the east coast. From taking the short commute through the tunnel for a concert in Central Park or a Broadway show whenever I wanted, to traversing Jersey's diverse landscapes of city, suburbs, farmlands, and down-the-shore haunts, and the occasional drives to Philly or DC, I never thought I was missing much. I'll be forever thankful for the cross-country drive to California that changed all that.

I developed a burning curiosity about people, places, economies, dialects, food, history, and more. Not only was it the start of my transition from a just-beginning legal career to a passion for journalism, but I also became hooked on travel, soon concluding that it was the greatest education one could attain. Notwithstanding our requisite degrees, career paths and life experiences, travel to me was all-encompassing. The lessons were profound and rich, the *Wow, I never knew that!* moments endless.

And so, when I retired more than forty years after that west coast drive and decided to move to Italy, I wasn't surprised by the excitement I felt at the prospect of embarking on this new adventure. I'd traveled to nearly fifty countries by then, and even lived overseas before, although never in the EU. And, even though I'd visited Italy countless times, I knew living there would be an entirely different experience.

The research and planning process, during a pandemic no less, yielded lessons that made my head explode on a regular basis, often not in a good way. But upon arriving in the place of my dreams to begin my final chapter, the challenges were dwarfed by the excitement of learning what my new life would look like—and how to even *do* life in this new place.

Mind you, it wasn't as if I walked around daily full of wide-eyed wonder and girlish glee. After all, I was still my old sixty-something curmudgeonly self. But it still felt good to learn new stuff. First experiences learning even mundane things like banking, post office procedures, queueing protocols at various establishments etc., were surprisingly exhilarating.

Sure, there was still the intimidation of walking into stores or government offices not yet having mastered the language. But, being reminded that there is always more to learn in life is so very validating. (Because, if there isn't, then what are we doing here?)

While being confused or even intimidated in new surroundings is common, I've always thought it best to guard against feelings of embarrassment or humiliation. You simply can't spend your life worrying about what others think of you or how they judge you. (And, when you reach retirement age, hopefully you've gotten past those concerns anyway, because there's just no time to waste on such nonsense.) When I made my big move, I had long since learned that, as long as you approach someone else's home country with respect, with anticipation and curiosity, rather than presumptuousness and entitlement, then you'll likely find that you'll reap what you've sown.

So, to heck with all that. The real issue is, what do *you* think of you? Are you feeding your soul and reaching your goals? Are you full? Are you happy?

Part of being a lifelong learner is always being open to knowing, understanding, and continuing to learn who *you* are. Not who you were thirty years ago, but who you are in each season of life.

I believe getting a good handle on this lesson is integral to finding success and happiness, not only as an expat in a new country, but in so many aspects of life. Because it was key throughout my journey, I'll discuss in these pages, from various perspectives, the importance of knowing yourself and what you really want (rather than what you may have wanted years ago, or what the world tells you you're supposed to want); liking yourself; and reaching life's decisions accordingly.

Of course, what being a lifelong learner looks like in different lives is a subjective thing. Getting to know yourself involves being honest with yourself. Some folks may just want to know all there is to know in their chosen field, or to work to become the very best of the best in a sport or hobby. For me, being a lifelong learner looks like everything, and moving to Italy was a reminder of this. Even things I don't necessarily want to know can grow me and expand my understanding of myself, of other people, and hence, of the world. The process is also humbling. Just when I think I've mastered something, or I finally get it, there's that inevitable *But wait, there's more!* moment.

If you're contemplating pursuing the expat life, you may find the process as exasperating and even exhausting as I did. Yes, there will be a lot to do, more than you can ever really anticipate or plan for. There will be rules and requirements that seem to make no sense. Or, maybe things will go a lot more smoothly for you. There is only one absolute guarantee that I can offer—it will never be dull.

* * *

What's In There?

Years ago, as a young widow whose only child had gone off to college, I lived and worked as a volunteer aboard a mercy ship. It was a Christian ministry whose mission was to deliver relief supplies to developing countries worldwide. I knew that for some crewmembers, it was an adventure and an opportunity to escape whatever cards life may have been dealing them at the time. For me, it was a calling. Sounds hokey, I know. But I believed, and still do, that each of us is put on this earth by a sovereign God for a purpose, and the early 90s was when I began to know that humanitarianism was part of the reason I am here. (Other parts included developing a love for great wine and great literature.)

From Big Brothers Big Sisters to volunteering with literacy councils and food banks, I always found the work revitalizing. But those were all works of service that could be accomplished in my spare time—not really that much of a sacrifice. The whole mercy ship thing involved leaving a comfortable career, selling my home, and for the first time not living in the country of my birth. Well, not living in any country, really. We were at sea half the time, and the remainder docked in nations around the globe, usually nations that were at war or recovering from war, fledgling democracies finding their footing after generations of communism or colonialism, etc.

After completing my initial two-year commitment, I left the ship and continued to work on the ground in Angola, whose unique status in the late 90s was that of both a former colony *and* a former communist country. At the time, Angola was not only figuring out what its first democratic government would look like, but still fighting off a bitter civil conflict at the hands of a terrorist rebel faction, as well as victimization by western countries who wanted to relieve it of its vast oil and diamond reserves. Interesting time to live in Angola.

Now, this is not some big pat on the back for being a selfless servant. After all, part of the reason I knew that humanitarianism was my "thing" was how it made *me* feel, so in some ways it was actually pretty selfish. And, while in Angola I also did some paid work for the AP and wrote for a couple of embassies (earning only a pittance, but still more than the checkpoint guards or the few remaining teachers whose salaries averaged $15 a week).

Looking back on those days of volunteerism, I realized I had learned things that I didn't even know I was learning until retiring in Italy.

It was fascinating how many people thought my time on the mercy ship was some exotic adventure, a never-ending vacation. After all, mercy ships were usually thought of as pristine hospital ships. This was not that. It was a dirty, greasy cargo ship, and my job as a galley cook involved long hours in the sweltering bowels of the vessel. The countries we docked in were full of horrendous sights and conditions that are permanently etched in my memory. As crew members, it didn't matter how we felt. It was a matter of doing a job—unloading the ship in 120-degree heat, talking and bargaining our way out of life-threatening situations, etc., etc. And gratification only came when the desperately needed food, clothing and building materials reached their intended recipients.

Gratification. Funny word. I guess I'd never given much thought to it before then. Not the same as being content with what you have or satisfied with what you've accomplished. It's that, yes, but much more. It's being full, at your soul's deepest levels. And those were the years I discovered fullness like I'd never known before.

I slept and dreamt that life was joy. I awoke and saw that life was service. I acted and, behold, service was joy.

Rabindranath Tagore

11

That wise Bengali Nobel Prize winner was on to something. Again, I realize you may be rolling your eyes right about now, but the concept is rooted in reality, probably much more so than you may think.

As a lifelong introvert, socially inept for as long as I can remember, it always seemed counterintuitive that I enjoyed entertaining. The time came when I realized what I really enjoyed was serving a meal I'd labored over, and then watching my guests savor and enjoy it. (Of course, I wanted them to leave as soon as they'd finished, so there was that.) And there was also the selfish element that was all about my own enjoyment. But their enjoyment had to come first. A perverse take on service, maybe, but it was service nonetheless.

The notion of giving while getting, and accepting that that was okay, turned out to be a central theme for me, not only throughout my career but it also occupied an important place on my roadmap to becoming an expat.

When I began my research, I knew little about NGOs or social service organizations in Italy, and I was probably ill-equipped to serve in many capacities anyway until I had a better mastery of the language. As a retiree and a freelancer, I would need to understand what service roles were available, and find the balance between being of service on my own schedule and getting some satisfaction out of the deal. Understanding that this would be an important, fulfilling part of my new life gave me a leg up in the planning process. I wanted to do something meaningful in my adopted country, but I also sought that selfish gratification. So, my research included scoping out opportunities that would meet that happy medium. Enter TEFL.

I learned that I could earn a TEFL (Teaching English as a Foreign Language) global certification that would qualify me to teach English abroad. The fact that I was so giddy with this discovery just confirmed that inherent need to do something that would benefit someone else—while not leaving *me* out of the equation.

In his memoir, Trader Joe's founder Joe Couloumbe coined the phrase *selfish altruism* to describe this concept. His stores were unique not only because of the fresh, healthy, and environmentally friendly fare, but because his employees were provided excellent compensation and benefits.

Yes, Couloumbe believed in the radical notion of actually caring about his employees and customers, but he was getting a lot out of the deal, too. For example, he explained in his book, by meeting employees' needs and reducing turnover rates, he increased his bottom line.

Keep in mind that acts of service can come in many different shapes and sizes. As a former journalist and now an avid consumer of journalism, I see the profession as a service, albeit a sometimes well-paid service (or so I'm told). It is among many professions that provide a vital service, often sacrificially.

Our adopted homelands need our support. If you are an aspiring expat, consider that this is what it means to become part of a community. It's not only about finding what's comfortable for you, and it should never only be about what they can do for you. What do *you* bring to the table?

As countries worldwide wrestled with the pandemic's effect on their economy, many U.S. consumers stepped up to try to support various industries, nonprofits and workers as best they could. This attitude should transfer to our new country. Whether on a temporary basis or going all-in and making a commitment to a service organization, it's worth searching out how you might get involved and perhaps make a difference.

One advantage to this search was that I got to know more intimately the demographics, needs, and inner workings of Italy's social structure. In his review of the Ron Howard documentary about Chef Jose Andres, film critic Ron Leydon wrote:

> *One is never at a loss to find places where there is good that needs doing in the world. And if you're actively searching, it's even easier.*

Knowing what's in us, what we have to offer, and what brings true fulfillment and gratification, may mean expanding our definitions and borders of understanding a bit. But, it's a wise starting point from which to enter any new season of life.

So, back to being an expat, and some of those questions I posed in the previous chapter. At your very core, what is it that feeds your soul? Where will you find *your* gratification? What I've tried to describe for you here are just a few keys in the process of knowing oneself. If you're thinking of embarking on a new life in some faraway land, these are mandatory considerations. The challenges that lie ahead are myriad, so you'd better know what you're doing. Which means you'd better know yourself.

Those same folks who may have thought I was off on some luxury cruise all those years ago on the mercy ship, had similar misconceptions about my new life as an expat. I heard countless comments like, *Did you hear, Carla's buying a villa in Italy,* or *Carla's moving to a vineyard in Tuscany.* Their mental picture was completely wrong. Of course, they had no understanding of what I was actually doing, nor did they need to. Everyone was happy for me, wished me well, laughed and joked during my virtual retirement party, and sent me on my way. And then there was one…me.

On the first day of waking up and realizing I didn't have a staff meeting but I did have a brand new laundry list of all sorts of things that I didn't really know how to do, the reality of what I *was* actually doing began to set in. It was the beginning of my two-month window before leaving the U.S.

While I never questioned or regretted my decision, and there was never fear of what lay ahead, there was nervousness and anxiety. There was plenty of racking my brain, certain that I'd forgotten something or missed something. And, when I thought about all there was still to be done, I felt overwhelmed. This is when I was thankful that I'd done the hard work of introspection to lay the foundation.

15

So, I encourage you to lay that same groundwork. Don't be afraid to look inside, find out what's really in there—and let it become your springboard.

* * *

Why? No, Really. Why??

We've begun to scratch the surface of what I call soul control—getting a handle on who you really are at your core, and setting out to become (and continue becoming) who you really want to be. These were the keys to how I began to design a blueprint for becoming a successful expat. But before I could move forward, there was another big question that warranted revisiting. Why?

Everyone wants to be as comfortable and carefree as possible, and yes, there are probably many expats who simply seek an escape to a do-nothing life of comfort and relaxation (nothing wrong with that, by the way). There are also those who just crave excitement, or anything different from the life they're living. And, of course, with the digital nomad phenomenon, the boom in remote working, and seemingly limitless expansion of tech startups, many employees and employers have a built-in reason to relocate. But I would venture a guess that, in every single case, there's more to the story. There certainly was for me.

You'll need to find out what your "more" is, because if you're not basing your decisions on the whole truth, you may be in for a rude awakening. This is important even if you're not retiring, but perhaps embarking on a sabbatical or an extended stay for work. Certain regions of the world may offer irresistible incentives and be ideal for your particular startup, but are they right for *you?* Even a year in a foreign place for all the wrong reasons (or not enough of the right reasons), and with all the wrong expectations, can end up being a terrible decision.

In an interview with journalist Bill Murphy, Jr., the restaurant chain Chick-Fil-A's executive director for franchisee selection, Maureen Donahue, shared one of many questions in the organization's criteria for new franchise owners. They ask, *Why?* More specifically, they ask, *Why do you want to own a Chick-fil-A franchise restaurant?*, over and over and over again throughout the months-long selection process. Murphy discussed Donahue's explanation:

> *"There are all kinds of layers that we can extract from that kind of a question," she told me. "We're always curious what they come to the table with, but definitely how the responses shift and mature. ... It actually becomes more profound in most cases, as they respond later in the selection process."*

Murphy continued,

Perhaps as much as any other interview I've done, this point has stuck with me. And, I've found myself quoting it lately. Sure, it's amusing that I found it while writing about Chick-fil-A, but this question strategy can benefit almost anyone making any big, important decision in life.

Most wise people at some point will ask themselves why they're doing what they're doing. Personally, I constantly check myself just to be sure I'm not acting in haste, in response to the wrong triggers, etc. After all, the whole idea behind tempting treats calling out to you at check-out counters is that there's no time to talk yourself down. I try never to take "bait" from advertisers or anyone else (or even from any of my own self-indulgent tendencies that may crop up from time to time).

But, asking yourself *Why?* over and over and over again, throughout an extended process, is a concept that stuck with me just as it did with Murphy. It's more than just a casual checking yourself and not letting yourself get out of hand. Particularly if there is no one else around to rein you in and help you honestly address times of ridiculousness, this process might be a great alternative.

Donahue shared that, more often than not, the franchisee applicants' answers evolved each time they were asked the question. Some even decided, late in the process, that they didn't want to be franchise owners after all!

Even though I read about the Chick-fil-A method after I'd made my decision to retire to Italy, I realized I'd already been employing a similar strategy. As events unfolded around me, as my introspection journey advanced, my reasoning took on new shapes and nuances. I was able to consider things I hadn't thought of before and, thankfully, each new realization seemed to validate what I was doing.

Keep asking why, even after the decision is made. You can always change your mind, whether out of fear or some newfound wisdom, or just a change in your circumstances. (Just be prepared for the consequences if you're already in too deep.)

When you continue to examine why you're making a life-altering decision, hopefully you'll find several cumulative, affirming reasons as I did. But, there may be one final straw, one main catalyst that pushes you over the line (or off the cliff, as the case may be). For me, that final straw was U.S. politics.

After years of traveling the world doing humanitarian work, covering news stories and just doing my thing, I had already begun toying with the idea of one day retiring in another country back in the early 2000s. Just a dalliance at first, since retirement was still a long way off. But there came a time, maybe a year or two before Covid, when events in the U.S. made me think… hard. With my country descending into what I saw as chaos, with racial tensions, rampant gun violence and political

partisanship on the rise, I realized I felt more
trepidation and anxiety about the future than I had
when living in a war zone in a developing country.

Retirement was approaching, and this time of
life was just not supposed to be this stressful. Even
if the then-president was not reelected, the band-aid
had been ripped off. The ugly mindsets and
worldviews, the divisions and the vitriol had been
exposed, and they weren't going away. (Of course
they'd always been there, but now folks had once
again been given license to be more open and vocal
about their feelings—i.e., to let their hate flags fly.)
I had to at least explore the possibility of a final act
somewhere else. Was this doable? Could it become
a reality?

I'd begun following *Dispatches Europe*, an
online publication written by and for expats, for
which I would later become a contributor. When I
read an article written as a guide to "getting out
while the gettin's good," I knew I wasn't alone. For
various reasons, but many under the same umbrella,
a great American exodus had begun. More and
more Americans were exploring the possibility of
living in another country. Beyond reasons for
leaving their home country, the article also helped
Americans understand the realities and some of the
advantages of building a new life in Europe:

- Strong social safety nets;
- Single-payer health care systems;
- Majority middle-class populations;
- Affordable undergraduate and post-
  graduate education;
- Safer streets and fewer guns; and,

- Generally healthier food choices and lifestyles.

And, there's so much more.

I'd always been a pragmatist, a researcher, and a doer rather than a dreamer. I would consider a matter at length, do my homework and, only when things came into focus and made sense, I would act. The day came when I looked around me and things began to come into focus. Most importantly, the idea *made sense.* And so began my journey.

So yes, there was one main catalyst for me, but again, I'd been kicking the notion around for several years, from several perspectives. Never should this be a knee-jerk decision, i.e., I love the food in Italy, so I think I'll move there for the rest of my life. It's a process, and it's probably best if you make it a pretty long process. As Murphy concludes in his Chick-Fil-A piece:

- *Ask yourself, "Why?"*
- *Ask yourself more specifically: "Why do you want this, in particular?"*
- *And most important, ask that question over and over and over again.*

* * *

Where In The World?

Knowing that I wanted to retire in another country, and having dissected and come to terms with my reasoning, deciding on the *where* was a no-brainer. Of all the countries I'd visited or lived in, only one called to me. The land of rolling hills and olive groves, the greatest art and the greatest wine, and culture, cuisine and history like none other. As a longtime Renaissance lover who'd spent an inordinate amount of vacation time in Florence, I knew if I was going to do this, then it had to be in Italy.

The decision came just as all those one-euro-home revitalization schemes were gaining momentum. Crumbling ancient villages all over Italy (and now in many other countries) were offering incentives to people who would come in and buy an abandoned property to restore, and perhaps even start a business there. Properties were being offered for the purchase price of one euro, with renovation costs that could really add up but were made more manageable through the government programs. Some municipalities were even paying young couples to move there and have babies.

While experiences varied with these initiatives, I was surprised to learn they were legitimate and many folks were reporting success stories. I read accounts of extended families getting together and buying up huge chunks of an entire village, etc. There were couples, young families and singles who jumped at the chance for a new start. There were descendants of former residents of some villages, who wanted to lay claim to generations of family history.

But, what works for one, may not work for another. I knew that renovating a dilapidated, abandoned home in a remote Italian village wasn't my cup of tea.

I realized the most important consideration had to be *me*, and not just what sounded like it would be a blast or a great deal. Would it work for *me?* This was a huge decision, and it was time to get real. I was a sixty-something retiree who would write, possibly teach, and hopefully stay fairly busy. I was also making the transition alone. I just couldn't be bothered with renovating a home in a foreign land. But there were other options, including shockingly affordable, move-in ready homes for sale, or renting, which made more sense anyway until I got my bearings.

Then there were the many other major considerations in choosing a location. This brings us back to the whole knowing yourself idea—your needs, your must-haves, what you can live without. How well do you know the culture, the lifestyle, the cost of living in the region you're considering? Are you willing to devote the time and effort needed to learn these things? Or will you simply expect everyone to adapt to *you?*

What about visas and residency requirements in your chosen country? And that whole new way of thinking involved in learning the metric system, if you haven't already done so. Are you prepared to begin counting and thinking in kilometers and kilograms, in military time, in euros rather than dollars? Do you have at least a basic grasp of the language?

(Being a "words" person and never having been a particular math whiz, I was surprised at how easily I adapted to the metric system, and how much more challenging it was to master the language. The things we learn about ourselves during the expat experience are endless!)

Also consider things like climate, etc. Are you prone to allergies? If the climate is not what you're used to, can you even live there comfortably?
After years of living in the dry, desert climes of New Mexico, at this writing I'm experiencing my first spring in Italy's Mediterranean climate. The humidity kicks in pretty early here, but thankfully, I've visited during past summer seasons, and also lived in humid U.S. climates before.

Taking these factors and more into consideration, I was very intentional about researching the things I loved about the place I was going, and reflecting on what I didn't love about the place I was leaving…and finding the balance.

Much of the basic information needed can be found on the internet, but verification is key. I found that there was *so much* information out there that some of it gave me pause. Although I gained valuable insights and helpful hints from experienced expats, I was reminded again that everyone's experience is different. Finding my way through such mazes as long-term visa requirements was monumental, and I often found conflicting information from different sources. Rules and regs were changing due to Covid, and many countries had begun requiring vaccination "green passes" at that time. But, governments were also becoming more creative with incentives, types of available visas, etc.

Bear in mind, my journey to becoming an expat was a retirement plan. There are many newly minted remote workers exploring living overseas, but my criteria were different. For example, I didn't need or want the regular hubbub of the big city, and I was careful to steer clear of tourist spots. But, I did need accessible public transport when I felt like getting out and about. Of course, reliable Wi-Fi is critical no matter your goals, and it was high on my list of must-haves.

Understanding housing costs, crime rates and accessible health care in different regions of Italy was also important. And I wanted a walkable and bikeable location with a train station, as I had no desire to ever own another car. When deciding where you want to settle as an expat, you must not only know your needs and wants, but obviously whether they are indeed available in your new location.

Choosing the town I wanted to call home was an enjoyable journey for me. Again, it was probably the whole learning experience that I loved the most. I learned good, bad, and surprising things about the country and its different *borghi* (villages). Although I'd traveled throughout Italy, this was my first time exploring where I could actually *live*. I first looked at furnished apartments and homes around the southwestern Campania region that were affordable and move-in ready. I also loved Tuscany—more expensive but not cost-prohibitive so long as I didn't want to live in the center of Florence. So, there were lots of options. But there was still so much more to consider.

It would be insane to move somewhere you've never been, or you've only been on vacation. Taking a couple of extended reconnaissance trips, staying somewhere off the beaten path, and getting to know the region and the locals in order to gauge whether it would be a good fit, are critical steps in answering the *where* question. Even if the region offers all of the amenities on your checklist, that doesn't mean you'll want to live there. As a Black American woman, I'm keenly aware that I may not be warmly welcomed everywhere I go. Then there are regions that simply may not want an influx of newcomers, no matter who you are. This is one key area where it's time to get real and take off the rose-colored glasses.

Never underestimate the importance of those recon trips. Sure, I knew I loved Tuscany, but this wasn't a movie and I wasn't one to romanticize things, anyway. I had to know if, and where, I would love *living* in Tuscany. So, it was crucial that I bum around a bit and get a feel for the locals.

At one point I found a village that I believed could be a great fit. For me, the appeal of Santa Fiora, population about 2,500, could be summed up in one word: quiet. This must-have was near the top of my list, and a very traditional, slow-paced village like Santa Fiora would meet the requirement perfectly. And they had one of the most original revitalization projects I'd seen. As part of the town's "Smart Village" project designed to attract remote workers, Santa Fiora had been equipped with high-speed broadband, along with internet cafes or "working stations." If accepted into the program, the town would pay a portion of my rent for several months while I settled in. Their hope was that once folks got a taste of the place, they would want to stay and buy property there.

And it was picturesque. Situated on a hilltop about 120 kms southeast of Florence, Santa Fiora's medieval piazza, frescoes and towers, not to mention the Peschiera reservoir and surrounding parks, were exactly what one might envision when dreaming of Tuscany. Rounding out the allure was its proximity to Montepulciano, known for some of Italy's best red wines, only about an hour away.

Once I learned that freelancing retirees were welcome in the program, and being the sucker—I mean informed researcher—that I am, I wasted no time in applying for Santa Fiora's Smart Village project. In their very gracious email response, the tourism bureau informed me that I must first secure a rental in town and then present my rental agreement and new address along with my application.

The requirement to have an address before being accepted into any initiative likely serves both the project and the fledgling expat. They want to know that you are serious, and you want to know what you're getting into. But, it also ended up being a hitch in several steps along my journey, including opening a bank account, securing medical insurance, and obtaining my long-term visa. It was almost as if you had to have a home in order to get a home.

Other towns and villages I got familiar with were not offering such incentives, and rentals weren't as complicated. One was Lucca, closer to Florence and practically next-door to Pisa. While most Tuscan villages sit on hilltops, Lucca sits at a lower altitude near the Serchio River. It was yet another medieval town with a fascinating history—founded by the Etruscans, meeting place of Julius Caesar, birthplace of Puccini, and still-standing city walls rumored to be designed by none other than da Vinci. Although the population was close to 90,000 with a tourist appeal that includes an annual Puccini Festival (thereby possibly robbing me of my coveted tranquility), Lucca was still worth a visit. It ended up being my new home of choice.

Just about every town I explored during those days was architecturally and culturally rich, some more touristy, some less. And no matter how small, they all seemed to have annual festivals.

Festivals are a mainstay of Italian culture, and one of the things that makes the culture so vibrant and fascinating to me. From tourist hotspots to the smallest villages, from the reverent to the raucous, these longstanding traditions celebrate food, wine, religion, art, music and film, not to mention epic gladiator battles. Even for those who treasure the quiet lifestyle, these events are irresistible.

All of these characteristics were appealing to me because they spoke to the rich history of the place. In nearly every case I also found a warm, safe, hospitable vibe. (Notice I said *nearly*. There is an important discussion to be had here, and I'll address it in the next chapters.) Rents were affordable, amenities and necessities accessible. Even in the most remote villages, there were neighborhood bars and restaurants, outdoor markets and busses or trains to Florence, Rome, etc.

Several years ago, on a bus ride from Florence to Pisa, I remember watching the rolling hills go by and wondering what life there was *really* like. Could it be as idyllic as it seemed? Just a fleeting curiosity at the time. (This was long before my decision to retire in the region.) In my present-day search I was even more curious, almost obsessively so. Enter that wide-eyed wonder.

Sometimes, when delving into exhaustive research, the skeptic in us looks for the bad as well as the good, at each turn wondering *what's the catch?* This, of course, is the wise approach, and I employed it throughout my planning and preparation for retirement in Italy. In my investigation of the land I planned to call home, I was pleasantly surprised to learn that there really was no catch.

For the most part, the country was exactly what it appeared to be, with little of the contrived nonsense we're all so used to. I attribute this partly to the fact that I did *not* approach the search wearing those proverbial rose-colored glasses. I tried to be very intentional about losing any unrealistic expectations or storybook fantasies I may have been harboring without realizing it. I was looking for what was real, for better or for worse.

As I got to know a few folks during my recon trips, I surmised that another reason for the authenticity I found was because the region is so old, and the small hamlets and villages that appealed to me wanted to keep things as they'd always been. They just couldn't be bothered with the cyber-predator, dog-eat-dog, fortune-amassing-at-all-costs culture of today. (Of course, that's not to say the mentality doesn't exist in the more modern regions that work hard to be a part of that culture just like the rest of the world.)

I'm eternally grateful that in many regions of Italy, the old traditions remain, the traditions that had always been part of the attraction for me. But, there are good old traditions and bad old traditions. While I chose to believe the good ones had been preserved just for me, I also kept my eyes peeled for the bad ones. And I wanted to know conditions and attitudes that might not be traditional, but just unique to certain villages, neighborhoods, or even individuals…

* * *

The House Hunt

Learning the ropes of apartment renting in Italy was fairly painless compared to other steps along my expat journey. In keeping with the national norm of a government that seems to care about its populace—*all* of its populace—the basic rental rules weigh heavily in favor of the renter, while also giving landlords decision-making latitude in writing their contracts. Most leases are long-term, usually a minimum of three years, providing protection from rent hikes.

A 3+2 lease, for example, means the initial term is three years and the lease renews automatically for two more years at the same rent with both parties' approval. The 3+2 and 4+4 leases are considered residential, a requirement to establish residency for some long-term visas, as opposed to the shorter transitory lease which is three to eighteen months. With your *codice fiscale* (a tax ID, similar to a social security number, which is required for nearly all business transactions), along with proof of income, you're good to go.

Of course, there's a caveat here for the new expat in Italy. Although long-term residential leases work in the renter's favor, obviously it's not a bad idea to first secure a shorter rental until you're sure you'll want to be there for years.

The very first flat I visited was in Lucca Province. The photos and description in the online ad depicted a furnished and rather spacious apartment, a huge plus given that most apartments in Italy are on the cramped side. It seemed to be equipped with everything I needed, and was located in a quiet area although still in the *centro storico* where I could walk to the train, shopping, etc. Being a somewhat newer building, there was even a lift, which I learned was a rarity in many older buildings, even those with three and four stories. The apartment itself seemed perfect, right down to the updated furnishings, private terrace and amazing view that I just knew would be conducive to good writing.

After texting with the landlord on WhatsApp over a couple of days, we made plans to meet at the apartment at 10:30 on a Friday morning. (This was one of the few apartments I found advertised through a private owner, rather than through an agency.)

I took the train from Florence and arrived at around 10:20. Nice looking building, just as pictured, but not a soul in sight. Not seeing any doorbells or other means of entry outside the gates, I texted the landlord announcing my arrival. No response. Looking up at the second-floor apartment, I saw no signs of life.

The woman had seemed delightful throughout our communications. We were both using Google Translate and shared jokes about its shortcomings. I'd concluded that she and her husband were millennials with young children. I knew they didn't live on the property since she had told me the most recent tenants had just moved out and she had been driving over to do cleaning and repairs. Maybe she was en route, behind the wheel and unable to respond.

After fifteen minutes I texted again. Are you coming to show me the apartment?

A woman walked out of the first-floor apartment. She looked about my age. *Buongiorno,* she said pleasantly. In my halting Italian, I told her I had an appointment to see the apartment above her, and asked if she'd seen the landlord. *No, mi dispiace.* We chatted for a few minutes and she told me how nice the building was and how sure she was that I would love it there. Getting a little ahead of herself, she asked when I would be moving in and even invited me to her place for coffee on moving day. Wow, even nice neighbors. This place just might be my new home!

Right about then—about 30 minutes after my scheduled appointment—a man emerged from the upstairs apartment and descended the stairs. He never smiled, but looked at me with disappointment and suspicion. He looked to be in his late 30s or so, with a set jaw and a bitter cold air about him. He and his wife had been there right along, no doubt observing me from the upstairs window. I clearly was not what they were expecting, and I knew immediately what I was dealing with.

Those of us who know racism first-hand recognize it when we see it. In fact, in the interest of self-preservation and survival, we can pretty much spot it a mile away. Whether in the States or anywhere in the world, the vibe is the same. Sometimes it's the suspicious side-eye, sometimes the hateful glare or the nervous politeness. People are people. Ignorance and hate are traits that are not limited to any one region of the world, and here again is where those rose-colored glasses must come off.

In her compelling 2018 New York Times essay, journalist Nicole Phillip described her year studying abroad in Italy. The school was in Florence, and she was one of several American students who had arrived together, roomed together and attended classes together. Phillip was the only Black student. Her experiences were harrowing—from having beer thrown on her and being called a "disgusting Black woman" while on a beach, to an elderly woman screaming and running away, to a millennial stepping in front of his girlfriend to *protect* her from Phillip, who had simply asked her for directions. And these were just a few of the more overt reactions to her very existence.

Phillip said she hadn't really known what to expect in terms of race relations in Italy, but she certainly didn't expect *that*. Even at home in the U.S., she described her mom's keen awareness of racism, while she herself sometimes had to have it pointed out to her—an oblivion that is unimaginable to those of my (and no doubt her mom's) generation.

Yes, Tuscany is an idyllic place for lovers of art, literature and good food and wine. But no matter how much you may love a place, at no time should you allow revisionist or idealist thinking to convince you there won't be racism, or many other ugly human characteristics. There will. Of course, we all have our prejudices, but that's different from the hate-filled racism that many people just don't realize is quite common. More prevalent in some places than others, certainly. But, in my many years of travels from the Americas to Europe to Africa to Asia, I have *never* found a place where it just didn't exist.

Back to those prospective landlords, who were certain I was going to rob and kill them. The husband led me into the apartment where the wife was waiting in terror. (She never did explain why she hadn't responded to my texts or why they'd left me standing downstairs for over 30 minutes. At that point, there was no need.) They grudgingly showed me around, going out of their way to discourage me at every turn, pointing out malfunctioning appliances and hoping against hope that I would not want to rent from them.

I didn't know what discrimination laws were in place in Italy, but I knew from countless stateside experiences that it didn't matter. As we've all seen, changing laws doesn't change hearts. Those ignorant dolts may have been legally obligated not to baselessly deny my rental, but I was certainly under no obligation to rent from them.

Not that I needed the wake-up call, but I was glad this experience was the first in my Italian househunting journey. Fortunately, it turned out to be the exception and not the norm.

So why, you may ask, would I want to live in a place where racism exists? It's a question I'd asked myself for years in the U.S. The answer, of course, is I don't. But, again, one would be hard pressed to find a place where it *doesn't* exist.

I've long believed that one of the most important words in the English language is *balance*. Sadly, in so many of life's circumstances, we must choose the lesser of evils. That's where research, planning, and weighing the good versus bad characteristics of your chosen home come in.

As beautiful as my surroundings are here in Italy, life's ugly realities are still here as well—but thankfully, much, much less so than I'd endured throughout the better part of my life before coming here.

* * *

The Global Grift

Having bummed around the *centro storico* for a couple of hours, both running errands and doing nothing in particular, I was about to head back to the flat. I'd been sitting in the park across from the train station, minding my business but keenly aware of my surroundings.

Seeing the man approaching me from the corner of my eye, I slid my phone into a pocket and looked up. I'd seen him hanging around the station several times before. Mid-30s, casually but neatly dressed in jeans, and with a confident gait, he greeted me with a big grin.

Lei parla inglese? Yes, I told him. My Spidey sense had already kicked in, but when he said he'd seen me earlier and wanted to be my friend, and could we exchange phone numbers, I became downright annoyed that he would interrupt my perfectly enjoyable day with this nonsense.

Okay, you little twerp, I thought. *Is it that you're that stupid, or do you think I'm that stupid?*

It was probably the latter. While many grifters are not the sharpest tools in the shed, others are brilliant in their chosen field, especially when they come across a willing victim. I was not the victim he hoped I would be. Once I put on my journalist's hat and began pummeling him with questions, he backed off.

Dismissing him out of hand and walking away, I had to wonder how many people fell for his schtick. There must be quite a few, or it wouldn't be worth the guy's time to keep at it. He would move on to another station, or perhaps a location near the airport, setting up shop just as a grifter would in any other country. As I'd seen several of his ilk around train stations throughout Tuscany, I knew they were just as plentiful here as anywhere.

As illustrated earlier, the ugliness of mankind, both moral and criminal, is not limited to any one country, region, age, ethnicity or gender. But, when it comes to being taken advantage of by grifters and scammers, I'm afraid many expats don't recognize this. Perhaps it's partly due to preconceived notions of what criminals look like. Or, the erroneous belief that these things just don't happen in the country where they've chosen to live.

I recently read an account of a young woman who'd lost over $300,000 of her inheritance in a crypto scam. She had fallen victim to someone she'd met on a dating site. When I read the story, I thought sarcastically that this was a case of double ignorance. But, a couple of days later, I saw the woman giving an interview on television. *Well, that took guts,* I thought.

The woman, who was of Asian descent and had been adopted as a child by American parents, detailed how the scammer had told her that he, too, was originally from the village of her birth. The connection was instant, and it wasn't long before he was sharing the miracle of crypto and the amazing investment opportunity he'd discovered.

With her mom having recently passed and bequeathed the family home to her, the woman had sold the house and wanted to start a new life. I had to wonder how much of this backstory she had posted on social media, or shared with her new online beau—too often the first step on the way down the scammer's rabbit hole.

Kudos to that woman for sharing her story in an effort to warn others. But, there have been countless warnings over countless years.

Of course, all manner of criminal, large scale and small, can be found in countries worldwide. Besides the well-known and rampant pickpocketing in tourist areas everywhere, there's corruption from CEOs and government heads on down; the petty thievery that often results from poverty and desperation; and, what I call "little kingdom" syndrome, i.e., folks like checkpoint guards in war-torn countries who control only the few square feet around them but rule that tiny bit of real estate with an iron fist. (I used to pay their bribery demands with food, not money.) But, the global grift is another story.

Anyone researching a new country to call home can be sure there will be disappointments. I doubt there is anywhere on earth that will live up to whatever idealized images we may have dreamt up. The same was proven true in my preliminary research of Italy, as well as after I made the move. But, the one thing that was exactly as I had read and expected was the country's low violent crime rate. All of my research touted Italy's safe streets and neighborhoods. (The low incidences of gun ownership and general hate and hostility certainly help in this regard.) Once I was settled, not only did I sense a safe vibe, but when I started to absorb local news, the reports were confirmed. Violent crimes are a small fraction of what larger western countries may be used to. And, I was pleased to learn that in many smaller Tuscan villages, violent *and* nonviolent crimes are almost unheard of.

However, many such encouraging stats may not be representative of the kinds of grifts that seem to be inescapable these days, in just about any country. These are often the kinds of criminals that don't make the local news. Shifty and elusive, their whereabouts as well as their numbers are often hard to monitor. For example, we all know that as soon as online scammers have been identified and shut down, or laws passed to hinder their activities, they just move on to a new scam. They always seem to be one step ahead of the law, and in our digital age, there seems to be no end to potential new enterprises.

It's demoralizing enough to be victimized in one's own country and language. But, in already unfamiliar surroundings, there may be an added sense of helplessness if we're not prepared. So, what's an expat to do? Perhaps just opening our eyes could be all the protection we'll need from the global grift.

The guy at the train station was clearly targeting Americans or other foreigners who might be on holiday or new residents in Italy. He had no doubt found victims who thought he was a clean-cut, friendly Italian man who just wanted to be helpful. How many of them had given him their phone number, connected with him on social media, and more? Had they really never seen a *Dateline* or *60 Minutes*? Had they heard none of those ubiquitous cyber theft and Ponzi scheme horror stories?

One common theme I've heard from people who have been victimized (and had the courage to come forward) is that they couldn't believe it had happened to *them*. They knew better. They *had* heard the stories, but had failed to heed the warnings. Oftentimes they were victimized by a supposed friend or, like the crypto scam victim, someone they'd met on a dating site.

There are also those who would never send money to some stranger on a dating site, but would indeed give their phone number to a total stranger on the street. And, while many wouldn't do such a thing in their home country, they inexplicably would in a foreign land.

Here is where all we really need is a little common sense—to stop and think for a moment. By what criteria do we deem someone trustworthy? Do they just *look* innocent enough? Too often, those folks who didn't think cyber theft, or even the old-fashioned in-person kind, could ever happen to

43

them, also rationalized that their attacker just didn't *look* like a criminal. They became victims of their own prejudices. (In the case of cyber theft, they were also victims of their own stupidity, because what are the chances that the photo posted online was really the person they were communicating with anyway?)

By definition, cyber crimes are accomplished virtually—through a device rather than in person. Our phones are computers, and we're connected worldwide. This, again, is common sense and not rocket science.

Even those like me who shun social media and would never share phone numbers or personal information with strangers, must be aware that thieves and grifters are finding their way around safeguards, even hacking into phones that are simply within a certain proximity. (And, for those of us who are technologically challenged and don't understand exactly *how* the scams and schemes all work, it's even more important that we recognize that they're out there—and they do work.)

While it's a sad truth that we sometimes must adopt the *trust no one* philosophy, it has served me well. From communications with rental agencies and proprietors of other businesses, to taking care to verify any information found online (even on government websites), the suspicion in me was probably one of my greatest protections during my early days in Italy.

So, this is just another reminder that recognizing certain of life's realities is an essential part of our preparation for the expat life. These realities must be grasped at home, and that awareness must accompany us to our new destination.

Arriving in a new country hopeful for a better life is a good thing. But, there are an awful lot of scammers, thieves and grifters, in every corner of the globe, who are awaiting your arrival, hopeful that it will mean a better life for *them*.

* * *

Timing Is Everything. Or, Is It?

There are no doubt many folks who reach a time in life when they set their sights on a particular change or adventure. They may even do all the research and planning, fully expecting that it will happen someday. But it never does.

Too often, the reason these people never pull the trigger is that it just never seems to be the right time. And, unless you have an employer mapping out your expat life for you, it likely never *will* be the right time.

At this writing we are seeing what we believe are the last gasps of the coronavirus pandemic (although it is now widely accepted as endemic, and there are currently a couple of brand spanking new Omicron subvariants). We are three months into the devastation that is the Russian invasion of Ukraine. As the war rages on, concern mounts around the world. Inflation is on the rise; gas prices are through the roof both here and in the U.S. (just as they were a few years ago, by the way). Two more mass shootings have occurred in the U.S., within days of each other. And, as anti-immigrant sentiment grows in the U.S., so it does in many parts of Europe, at least toward some immigrants.

What has been is what will be, and what has been done will be done again; there is nothing new under the sun.

Ecclesiastes 1:9

Will there ever be a perfect time, or even a "right" time, either in your new country or the one you're leaving? The pandemic ends, the war begins. You may not be hated for the color of your skin, but someone, somewhere, will resent you for something else, perhaps the company you work for, or your affiliation with a political party or just some other fly-by-night group. If you're accepted today, you may not be tomorrow. If you're financially comfortable today, you may not be tomorrow. How will you determine which of these factors will be the defining one, the one that says, *wait,* or even *now's the time to go*?

You can make yourself crazy weighing all the variables. At the end of the day, you simply cannot know the future. Becoming an expat should neither involve snap decisions nor waiting for the perfect time. You simply must work with the tools you have, the foremost being wisdom.

In Italy, for example, the legislation voting into law the Digital Nomad Visa for non-EU citizens was finally signed as of March 2022. This comes years after other European countries took the lead in offering the incentive to remote workers. And, while Italy initially proposed this visa back in early 2020, it is only now becoming a reality. One can only hope that the country's notorious bureaucracy won't delay things further. (There are already qualification questions, since the law as currently written requires *highly qualified work activities, suitable accommodation,* and *adequate income*, among other conditions already needed for all visas. Specific definitions have yet to be provided.)

Those who may have been hoping to get on the digital nomad train in 2020 and may have made the mistake of thinking things would move along quickly (during Covid, at that), are probably still waiting.

One incentive in which Italy did take the lead was its one-euro-home program, offered in various forms throughout the country. That initiative was also affected by Covid, along with other unexpected factors. Noted Australian chef Danny McCubbin purchased a one-euro property in Sicily and tried for months to find builders to complete the needed renovations. He found that there was a shortage of builders due to a new government tax break for homeowners on eco-friendly renovations and upgrades. So, everyone had immediately grabbed up all the builders and other contractors.

Unable to complete his renovations within the required window, McCubbin ended up selling his home back to the government for the same one euro he'd paid for it. But, undaunted, he bought another home in Sicily for eight thousand euros and found builders to do the minor needed fixes for a few thousand more. Today, he runs *The Good Kitchen*, a community kitchen that prepares and delivers free meals to vulnerable families in the town of Mussomeli.

McCubbin is an example of someone who understood that one can always find reasons to wait, but chose to let wisdom rule the day. He wanted to purchase a home in Italy; despite obstacles, he not only found a way forward for himself, but in the devastating dynamics associated with Covid also identified a need that he could fill for others.

In addition to world events like wars or pandemics changing life as we know it, laws, rules and regulations, and tax structures can change at the drop of a dime. *Anything* can happen that might necessitate regrouping. The question is, will we in fact regroup, or will we just stop?

Determining my *when* wasn't too difficult for me. In fact, retirement was actually my first calendar marker. More difficult than deciding when to move to Italy was deciding when to retire, i.e., at 70 years, at "full" retirement age of 66, or two years early at 64. I took the time necessary to reach a wise and pragmatic decision, and moved forward.

After the retirement decision, the only question in terms of the move was whether there was sufficient reason *not* to do it right away. Waiting would mean continuing to endure those negatives that were so unpalatable to me in the U.S., as opposed to the healthier lifestyle, more manageable cost of living, and cultural appeal that drew me to Italy. I concluded there simply was no reason to wait. I had come to terms with the things I loved and would miss about my home country, and the decision had been made. That is, barring any legal restrictions, what with the new virus that was spreading around the world at breakneck speed.

Of course, what came next was the earsplitting screeching of brakes. I wouldn't be going anywhere, any time soon. All my plans went out the window, but for me that only meant regrouping, *not stopping.*

While Covid made us all forget most of our inconsequential issues, this was a big deal. I had to somehow try to keep moving forward. Yes, the travel restrictions prevented me from checking off many of the boxes on my many to-do lists. Folks could barely plan getting next week's groceries, let alone relocating to another continent. But I pressed on. While I couldn't ignore the reality of Covid, and even the possibility of contracting it, I saw no sense in waiting. For what? There was no way to know how or when we would see the end of a novel virus that even scientists knew little about.

The benefit of added time that came with being homebound meant there was no limit to the thoroughness of my research. But there was added frustration that came along with it. The EU and its individual countries like Italy were in the same boat as the U.S. in terms of mapping out a way forward. And, because Italy had one of the highest case counts in the world in those early days, my mission was more difficult than ever. Still, the alternative of waiting (and doing nothing) just wouldn't work for me.

Interestingly, even though borders were closed and international air travel was, for all intents and purposes, nonexistent, airlines were still taking reservations for future flights.

So, in February of '21, when Italy and the rest of the world was locked down with no relief in sight, I went ahead and booked a reconnaissance trip for November. Yes, it was a crapshoot, but everything was refundable and flights were dirt cheap at that time. And the gamble paid off. Despite the raging Delta variant, just when I needed it to, Italy opened its borders. Of course, there were innumerable hoops to jump through, like mandatory masking and vaccines, and those long, detailed passenger locator forms that had to be filled out for each country I'd be traveling through. Travel at the time was not for the faint of heart. But, I had chosen my *when*. All that was left was to decide whether or not to be discouraged by the circumstances of the day—a decision that we get to make for ourselves, and one that no one can make for us.

Those who have spent a lifetime having decisions made for them, and particularly those whose careers haven't included making departmental decisions for subordinates, for example, may struggle here. I've met folks whose fear of retirement was not because they weren't financially prepared, or didn't want to lose their coworker connections, but based solely on the what-ifs.

Similarly, people who desperately want to make a move or a change in their lives often don't because of the unknowns. Interestingly, these are often the same people who, while waiting for who-knows-what to happen, don't seem willing to take steps to *make* anything happen of their own choosing.

For those who opted for that wait-and-see route, I have to wonder how long they waited. And, after all was said and done, what did they finally see?

Looking back, I'm so very glad I didn't wait. What would I have waited for? Things to change? What things? Or, for there never to be another challenge, another virus, another war or economic downturn?

If you've decided that the expat life is for you, let wisdom, not circumstances, rule the day when choosing your *when*.

* * *

Preparing to Get Prepared

Once I had kinda, sorta put together the *who, what, why, where and when* puzzle pieces of my adventure, and armed myself with tons of research and reality checks, I was pretty tickled at the prospect that I might really be ready to do this. Or, at least, I felt equipped to begin getting ready. But I still had no real understanding of the logistics still to be worked out.

Logistics is generally defined as the detailed organization and implementation of a complex operation. In military science, logistics deals with the procurement, maintenance, and transportation of military material, facilities, and personnel. Not long after I arrived in Italy, I heard a roundtable of talking heads discussing the war in Ukraine. One of the participants, retired Admiral James Stavridis, caught my attention. The former NATO Supreme Allied Commander definitively stated, *Professionals are focused on logistics; the amateurs are worried about the strategy. Logistics eats strategy for lunch.*

It's a concept that is worth considering in the planning of the complex operation of becoming an expat. Perhaps strategy is simply the big idea of deciding where you want to live (a rental or a purchased home, in a particular region of a particular country); how you'll support yourself (remote work/startup/pension); and, when you will make your move. Logistics, then, would be figuring out the detailed organization and implementation of this complex operation--the rules and regulations, required forms, documents and timetables. If you're not well prepared, the logistics of this bureaucratic maze will eat your big idea for lunch.

But, it's hard to prepare for something that is unfamiliar to you, in an ever-changing environment that is even more unfamiliar. As a citizen of just about any country these days, you can find out anything you need to know, no matter how unfamiliar it may be, where your own homeland is concerned. For example, when I retired, I had to learn the ropes of Social Security, Medicare, etc., including taxes, health care premiums, and so much more. But, all the information I needed was readily accessible. (A pain in the neck, but it was there.)

Figuring out laws and customs and protocols in a language that you're just beginning to get comfortable with, and in a place that you've never lived before, is another story. My first big challenge was not so much about getting to Italy, or what I wanted to do when I arrived, but obtaining the legal right to stay here.

After researching the many different types of visas available for those who want to visit long-term or live in various parts of Europe, I realized there was even more soul-searching to be done. The Digital Nomad Visa was already available in several countries. It was all the rage because of all the remote work opportunities in technology and other fields. But Italy's Elective Residence Visa that I was interested in was only for those who were, for all intents and purposes, independently wealthy. You're not allowed to work to support yourself, but must be able to subsist on pension, savings, investments, etc.

There were a couple of full-time gigs I had considered, but this changed pretty quickly for many reasons, some practical and some because I just wasn't sure I *felt* like being an employee again. The practical reasons included the fact that I was already drawing Social Security and there was a limit to the additional income I could earn. I just wasn't sure I wanted to change my status.

As is the case in just about any endeavor, financial concerns often top the list of priorities for expats. It's imperative to understand the cost of living, your tax status, etc., while living abroad.

During my research, I met a couple of young aspiring expats who were also freelancers. Their earnings were still quite meager at that point. They were disheartened to learn that the IRS had decided to demand records from PayPal, Venmo and Zelle, for the purpose of taxing anyone earning over $600. The couple was young and therefore had no pension and little savings—they were completely dependent on freelance careers that were still in the early stages. As the woman told me, it wasn't that they didn't want to pay taxes on their earnings. They were just a little miffed about how the government was going about collecting those taxes. They found it astounding that the U.S. government saw fit to hunt down the babysitters and dogwalkers typically paid through these apps for their measly $600, while millionaires continued unchecked in their Trumpian ways of paying little to no income taxes. (Really, IRS?? But I digress.)

I learned that taxes can be quite high in Italy, but that it was a worthwhile tradeoff. It wasn't difficult to see that taxes actually work for the taxpayer here and never would I wonder where all that money was going. There were also substantial tax breaks for retirees in certain regions, but Tuscany was not one of them. Understanding all of these factors was key in determining if long-term or permanent residency was for me.

The research required to even decide which visa I should apply for, and then learn how to apply for it, was draining. This was a critical part of the preparation process, and it helped me to understand that it was important to be prepared to even get prepared. You may think you have all your ducks in a row and your grand plan will move along swimmingly, but there will always be unexpected twists and turns.

There was that twist of having to have an official, registered residence before I could even apply for a visa (actually, I learned this was a requirement before I could proceed with many things). This would mean at least one additional reconnaissance trip just for househunting.

Another requirement for my residence visa was health insurance. This is an area where lots of expats start out with the wrong idea. Many believe that, because of the EU's much-lauded universal health coverage, there's no need for medical insurance. False. It's not only needed but required for expats until they acquire their residency—but it was also very easily attainable with a little online research. And, together with the universal health care, the cost amounts to a tiny fraction of health care costs in the U.S.

My countless hours of research yielded many more discoveries, and each time I learned of some new rule or requirement, my timetable shifted. But my little old retirement-in-Italy delays couldn't hold a candle to Covid.

I remember reading about people who'd planned weddings, quinceañeras or new business ventures for years, only to have all those plans dashed when the world shut down. Some of these stories were heart-wrenching; they also served as a reminder that my move to Italy being delayed was not the end of the world. These were times and circumstances that no one could prepare for, uncharted waters on a journey that we were all making up as we went. But hopefully, we learned a lot.

During the pandemic, the logistics of the expat operation had to be carried out in cooperation with certain mandates, etc., not to mention the same delays and cancellations that people were experiencing in other activities. Governments were scrambling to devise new online forms and regularly update statements on embassy websites. Once the vaccine became available, there were requirements to prove you'd been vaccinated before doing just about anything. Entering some countries was still banned altogether.

To cope with frustrations like the flights for one of my recon trips being cancelled (and this after more than a year of delays while not being able to fly at all), I again employed the old practice of accentuating the positive. I began to see Covid and all its woes as a microcosm of life, a mini university course in wise planning and flexibility. I tried to take advantage of the extra time for research, and I was thankful to learn a few things that I wouldn't have known I needed to know, had I been able to forge ahead earlier. I was reminded not to be surprised at anything, and to have a backup plan for everything (like having travel insurance to cover the possibility of testing positive for Covid while on a recon trip, and then having to quarantine in a foreign country). So many things in life are one big gamble, and sometimes you'll just have to drop back and punt. You pays your money, you takes your chances.

Another glaring lesson that many folks learned during the pandemic was that they weren't special. Most of us who were preparing for our new lives as expats, or just making travel plans for whenever the world opened up, just took our lumps and adjusted our schedules. But there were others who would have none of learning this lesson.

Back in the days of living in Angola, small groups would occasionally visit from the States to "help" me in my work. I was always amazed at the inherent thinking that they were indeed special, so they could ignore societal norms, condescend to the locals, etc., even though I had sent them thorough educational guidelines beforehand.

In planning the aforementioned recon trips, I had to research the mandates and restrictions not only of Italy but any layover countries as well. In other words, I had to *prepare* to comply with rules that were constantly changing. During the trips, it was beyond disappointing to see people in airports (sadly, often Americans) loudly objecting to mask requirements, etc. Of course, I knew this was happening in the U.S. But, surely these travelers had done the same research as I had. Such planning and preparation was not just a good idea in those difficult days of Covid travel—it was imperative. So, in their planning, did their privileged thinking just conclude that the rules did not apply to them?

I learned it was also becoming a common occurrence for unvaccinated people to vocally express their indignation at having to quarantine upon arrival in a new country—even after they'd signed the required forms acknowledging that those were the rules and they would abide by them. I was hard-pressed to understand why they would agree to protocols that they knew full well they had no intention of adhering to.

I suppose for the special, privileged few, planning and preparation just won't matter, and no lessons will be learned. They may have strategized a big idea of living in another country, but given no thought to the necessary logistics. But the rest of us can find those pandemic lessons to be valuable takeaways to pack in our logistics toolkit. As an aspiring expat, they certainly came in handy for me.

* * *

The Human Factor

There was a time, when traveling to developing countries or those with differing political ideologies than the U.S., that getting a visa to enter the country was quite a challenge. But, in recent years as I've traveled for vacation far more often than for work, my destinations have primarily been countries that don't require visas for stays of up to ninety days. With the decision to relocate to Italy for permanent (or at least long-term) residency, my visa once again became my biggest concern.

Once I began to delve into what was required and what was available to me, every element of the visa question seemed to loom over me, from which type of visa I would need to managing the paperwork and the timing, dotting all the I's and crossing all the T's. During the process, I was constantly reminded that while I was focused on my feelings and wants and needs, all I was to the authorities was a stamp in a passport.

I harkened back to those days of angry, accusing customs people demanding to know why I was traveling to their country. (In a country at war, such suspicion was justified.) I remembered incidents in certain countries where I'd been pulled out of customs lines, detained and told that my visa was bogus, or other countries where my belongings were taken away for no apparent reason. So, probably flirting with a little PTSD, applying for my Italian visa was a bit daunting and sometimes pretty emotional. As I studied blogposts and articles written by established expats, I learned that some had found the process straightforward; others said it was unnecessarily involved, but not difficult. I wasn't too happy about the bureaucracy everyone reported, but I overcame some of the jitters and was convinced I could do it, without hiring an immigration attorney.

Every aspiring expat should prepare for the bureaucratic quagmire often involved in obtaining a long-term visa. I've already mentioned it several times simply because it was such a major part of the process, but it's worth emphasizing again. Of course, your experience will depend on your chosen country, and sometimes on which side of the bed your consulate representative got up on. I'll detail here just a few of the steps that I had to navigate.

While Italy offers various types of long-term visas (for more than 90-day stays), only the Elective Residence Visa is specifically designed for retirees or those who do not plan to work while in Italy. In fact, working to earn the required income is forbidden under this visa. The applicant must be able to show a minimum annual income (currently about 32,000 euros) deriving from social security, pension, savings and investments. It's a strict and inflexible requirement, but understandable in that the country simply wants to ensure the new resident will be self-sufficient.

The Elective Residence Visa application must be submitted to the appropriate Italian Consulate in one's home country, *before* the permanent move to Italy. My home in the U.S. was under the jurisdiction of the Consulate in Los Angeles, and I was granted an appointment within a reasonable time—that is, after numerous errors occurred when the site attempted to process my request.

In addition to specific forms of proof of income and the completed application (which can be downloaded from the Consulate's website) other required documents included a valid passport; two recent passport-size photos; a lease contract or other evidence of an address in Italy (the contract must be registered with the government); and, proof of health insurance with at least a one-year coverage period.

I was very careful to have all my ducks in a row before my appointment, and tried to anticipate the unexpected based on the experiences of other expats. The process was not without its headaches. The consulate representative was rude and condescending, and I was not granted the visa on the first try due to a very minor technicality. But, after clearing up one documentation error, the end result was my passport being returned in a timely fashion and my being able to return to Italy to finally begin my residence, visa in hand. But, there's more.

Once my visa was obtained, the next requirement was to apply for the *permesso di soggiorno,* which is essentially the permit that supersedes the visa. This must be applied for within eight days of arriving in Italy.

Again, the Elective Residence Visa is unique. Although it was the only one suitable for my particular situation, there seems to be a visa for everyone wanting to relocate to Italy, whatever the reason—business/employment, study, military dependent, sports, religious/mission, and more. While I don't know if these visas carry the same strict requirements, I was amazed to learn of all the options. I thought back to the old challenges of entering various countries, and of the current challenges being faced by many.

While my heart broke for the Ukrainians fleeing their war-torn country, I was thankful that they were welcomed with open arms into just about any nation they chose, temporary and even long-term visas being offered readily.

I was one hundred percent supportive of the Ukrainian immigrants, but I was also saddened at the thought of the millions of people, some whom I've interviewed or known personally over the years, who fled various atrocities in their own countries, only to be turned away, denigrated, imprisoned or worse when trying to enter a new country. Memories of these souls will be with me always.

Sarah Nagaty is an Egyptian PhD student of cultural studies based in Portugal. In a series of articles for *Dispatches Europe,* she discussed being an expat, an immigrant, or "falling between the cracks:"

> *I, for example, as well as a Palestinian friend of mine, have our lives defined by the necessity of applying for European Union citizenship (for safety and protection in our home countries) which sounds horrendous or opportunist or "poor you" by expat standards as they definitely make choices in life on different grounds.*
>
> *However, this limitation would also sound like a luxurious problem compared to our friends who were never granted visas to travel outside their home countries or those who are arbitrarily spending their youths in Arab prisons.*

Whether you're a retiree, a student, a soldier, a freelancer or employer/employee, you will be assigned a label in the eyes of your new country. Your label is determined by the country from which you hail, or the activity in which you're engaged. When applying for the Elective Residence Visa, your bankbook determines your worthiness.

We're actually all immigrants in our new land, whatever our label. You may think of yourself as an expat, which sounds a little softer, but there is really no human factor involved. I've discovered that the one common denominator among many of us is that no one wants to hear our story. A hard truth, but unavoidable.

For me, this reality was just that--reality. Like Nagaty, the key was to find the balance and accentuate the positive. Coming to terms with these aspects of the expat life was simply a part of the journey.

* * *

Connecting

Consider some of the everyday things we purchase or subscribe to, apps we download, accounts we open, etc. We take such transactions for granted these days—that is, unless their costs increase or something better and shinier comes along. Opening accounts like banking, utilities and phone service is pretty commonplace in one's home country. Many of us maintain the same accounts for years on end, and may not even be up to date on current procedures should we need to open a new one.

When establishing services in a new country, it may be a whole different story. Such fundamentals of everyday life can get quite complicated.

Some may prefer to secure legal representation to do the heavy lifting for them, establishing all of their initial services and only requiring the expat to sign on the dotted line. Expat lawyers who are well-versed in these processes can usher you through the labyrinth. They are readily available and easy to find online or through other expats, although their fees may be a little difficult to swallow. What with my innate hostility toward bureaucracy and red tape of any kind, and still reeling a bit from the visa hoops I was jumping through, I was very much tempted to hire one of these advocates. But the frugal side of me chose to wait. If things got too complicated, I could always hire an attorney later, but I decided to first attempt to schlep through the mire on my own.

The simplest of these processes was establishing cell phone service. Because I knew it would be important to keep in touch with people back in the States, maintain my stored contacts and data, *and* have WiFi and other services in Italy, I was initially concerned that the whole process would be yet another maze. It was not.

During my first couple of months in my new country, I was adamant about wanting to keep my American phone number. I had researched the best ways to obtain service through an Italian company, but I was in no hurry. I kept my old AT&T account during that time, until I got my feet wet.

Despite my aversion to social media, a friend had convinced me months earlier of the advantages of WhatsApp, and I'd already been using it for quite a while to communicate with friends and colleagues abroad. So, during the initial period I communicated only through email and WhatsApp. This was a good plan for those early days, allowing me to text and have audio and video calls with family and friends. But then the time came to figure out my Italian connection. I wanted to keep my existing phone but have an Italian phone number. (I probably would never have admitted it back then, but this was for more than just practical reasons. Deep down, I somehow thought it would be validating, that I might feel just a little more at home with the same country code as everyone else. I was right.)

Purchasing a SIM card to use with my existing phone was the easiest way to cover all these bases, and yet still was not a permanent commitment. While I had never done so during past travels, once I learned how SIM cards worked, it was the obvious choice.

The miniscule memory cards connect you with local phone service, get you "into" the system and enable the provider to set up your account, while maintaining the info and data already stored in your phone.

With numerous phone providers in Italy and throughout Europe just as in the U.S., it's a good idea to do the same comparison shopping that you've probably always done, to be sure you're getting the best plan to meet your needs at the most reasonable price. The three major companies in Italy are Wind Tre, Vodafone and Telecom Italia. I found their prices to be comparable and, once you're settled, each also offers internet services. Again, knowing your needs and shopping around will be key.

Speaking of needs, another advantage to purchasing a SIM card as opposed to going all in and buying a new phone and permanent service, is the ability to change your mind. New expats *need* this option. As is the case with an apartment lease agreement, it's best not to make long-term commitments until you know what you're getting into.

Before establishing even temporary phone service, Italy requires that you have a *codice fiscale.* This is an identification code necessary for tax purposes and to "legitimize" you as an actual person. Although it's one of the most critical requirements for opening accounts, establishing services, etc., in my experience obtaining the codice fiscale was also one of the easiest processes. Application can be made either at a local *Agenzia delle Entrate* (tax office), at the American Consulate in Italy, or the Italian Consulate in your home country. The number is issued immediately, and the card is mailed within a few weeks.

Once you have your codice fiscale in Italy, purchasing a SIM card requires only a photo ID. You can walk into a phone store just about anywhere and get started. However, it's best to steer clear of the stores in airports, as they're known to be notorious price gougers. Likewise, although SIM cards can be purchased online, it's hard to know what you're getting—and whether it's even legal.

While I discovered there were several reasonable phone plans available, I initially opted for one offering pay-as-you-go service. Once my ten-euro activation fee was paid, my monthly bill averaged the same amount. The plan allowed me to monitor how much data I was using and, if I was nearing my limit, to "top off" or add money to the account if needed.

The process I'm describing applies to Italy, but it is likely similar in other EU countries, as most of the major phone carriers operate throughout the region.

The SIM card is probably a no-brainer for those who aren't dinosaurs like this writer. When I learned that many of the 2022 Olympians had opted to used SIM cards while in China, I wasn't surprised. Because other steps in my journey had been overwhelming, I fully expected staying connected in a safe and secure way, without any initial long-term commitment, would be one of the most challenging tasks. But, for me, this was a convenience that I saw as a modern marvel, a delightfully uncomplicated breath of fresh air in my expat experience. Even the most tech-averse travelers and new expats can be thankful for the SIM card.

There are so many trial-and-error decisions required of new expats—daunting because there's just no way to know if you've made the right choice. Fortunately, phone service doesn't have to fall into that category. It is one of those rare times in life when you get to ease into your decision until you're comfortable, and even then, you can hang on to your options. If things don't work out, just pop your original memory card (and number) back into your phone and be on your merry way.

* * *

Quanto Costa?

The big, overarching relocation question, whether at home or abroad, is usually *how much?* We hear varying commentaries on how much cheaper it is to live here or there, but, as with every other aspect of this endeavor, it's all subjective. So, although my story may provide new expats with a general idea of what to expect, it should be taken with a grain of salt.

There came a time, about a year or so before my retirement, when I realized something I'd previously taken for granted. It was the fall of 2020 when everyone was trying to figure out how to "do" the holidays in that first year of Covid. Someone asked me what I wanted for Christmas. I couldn't think of a single thing that I wanted.

Long before that, I'd started designating long stretches (one month, three months, six months) of not making any purchases for myself except food and personal necessities. As those time periods increased, the lifestyle became second nature. So, by the time that first pandemic Christmas came along, it occurred to me that there was virtually nothing I needed and, more importantly, not a single material thing that I wanted. I spent the entire following year giving away nearly everything I owned.

Again, no big pat on the back here. I've talked to several people who made similar decisions during the pandemic. The virus changed us all, sometimes in the most unexpected ways. (And this coming from a one-time clothes horse and shoe addict.)

What matters is the lasting effect, and most folks I spoke with, like me, had decided to embrace this new minimalist lifestyle for good. I had lived for a couple of years in Angola with virtually no material possessions, but this time it was a *choice.* And it held particular importance in terms of a new life in a new country. As I researched Italy's cost of living, I realized this move was going to be a very, very good thing financially.

Beyond just not requiring a bunch of material things, there was also my diet. As a pescatarian who had adopted the Mediterranean diet years before it became all the rage, my grocery bill was just a nominal expense. Overall, I already had a very low cost of living, even in the U.S. All that I had read confirmed the general cost of living in Italy to be much lower than that of much of the U.S., so I was pretty confident when I began to create a budget.

Economists and other financial experts generally agree that the average cost to live in Italy can be from 15% to 30% less expensive than living in the U.S., and even less expensive than that in certain regions. Of course, like anywhere in the world, the cost of living in Italy varies depending on a number of factors, location being only one. It should come as no surprise that living in a bigger city or tourist hub will be more expensive. But even there, Americans will be astonished to learn how affordable it is.

Rome and Milan are known to be two of the most expensive cities in Italy. While life in these cities is said to be comparable to living in New York, I personally don't believe they've quite reached such exorbitant costs as those in the Big Apple just yet.

Florence, the center of Tuscany and the cradle of the Renaissance, is also a tourist hub and therefore can be fairly costly, relatively speaking. Surrounding towns and villages are not. And, although the popularity of the Tuscan region where I live does indeed make it somewhat more expensive than, for example, the southern regions of Abruzzo, Puglia and Calabria, it will still not be cost prohibitive for most Americans.

With those general parameters in mind, below are some of the everyday costs associated with my low-key lifestyle in Italia:

- I spend about 40 euros per week on groceries. One liter of milk is less than one euro; my favorite salmon fillets are about two-thirds of what I paid in the U.S.; fresh produce, along with the best olive oils and wines in the world, are also much less than what they would cost elsewhere.

- Rents for one- or two-bedroom flats around Tuscany can cost as little as 500 to 600 euros per month, and even less in the southern regions.
- Compared to rents, utilities can be expensive. I am fortunate enough to have landlords who were willing to negotiate a monthly rent that would include utilities and WiFi. Such rental contracts are not uncommon, but generally speaking, tenants are expected to pay for electricity, gas and water. While utility costs also vary by region, an average household may pay a total of 175 to 250 euros per month for all three of these services.
- WiFi is available from several providers, at an average cost of 30 euros per month.
- Fuel is expensive in Italy, with gas prices currently skyrocketing due to the war in Ukraine. Not being a driver here, I purchase a monthly pass that can be used on any bus or train, for about 35 euros per month. (A word here about public transportation in Italy: Because I hadn't used public transportation in the U.S. since my east coast days forty years ago, I had no real frame of reference for what it would be like to be dependent upon it in everyday life. For me, the modern efficiency, cleanliness and overall structure of public transportation in this country is nothing short of amazing.)
- The healthcare system in Italy is known as one of the best in the world. Although I

thankfully have not yet had to access it, I've heard glowing reports from other expats. Once you are a resident, you can join the national healthcare plan. However, even when you're eligible to do that, you may want to keep your private insurance if you want a personal family physician and quicker access. I purchased an international insurance plan for $1200 per year.

- Entertainment costs are generally comparable to the U.S., but eating out is less expensive. A full-course restaurant meal (outside of the tourist spots) can cost as little as 12 euros; a decent Chianti as little as 4 to 5 euros per glass; and, a cappuccino for about one euro.

- As mentioned earlier, taxes can be quite high in Italy. Income taxes (including on international retirement pensions), as well as property taxes for those buying a home, should be carefully researched. This is one area where it may be well worth the cost of that immigration attorney.

Of course, all of these average costs apply to the weird times in which we find ourselves at this writing in mid-2022. Any mature adult in any nation on earth knows there will be inflation, boom-to-bust markets and economic fluctuations. There will be wars, and even pandemics.

One of the built-in gauges I was able to use when budgeting for my new life was the minimum monthly income requirement for my Elective Residence Visa. As a retiree on a fixed income, and based on my modest standard of living and the average costs I'd researched, I knew I would be able to live more than comfortably in the Tuscan town I chose to call home. (Barring drastic changes in the world economy, that is.) If you're still in the workforce, possible changes in your job status and compensation of course must be considered.

We all know that budgeting is always a crapshoot, and perhaps more now than ever. Budgeting for life in a new country is even more stressful. But, because many EU countries, including Italy, have a low cost of living as well as carefully thought-out social protections in place, it may be less risky and less stressful to plan these financial aspects of your expat life.

I've tried to cover some of the most basic costs of a life here in Italy, but of course these are just averages that apply to one person's lifestyle. My experience, however, is a good example of a country that is as affordable as it is beautiful. I find myself singing Italy's praises a lot since I've been here, and the cost of living ranks high on my long list of positives.

* * *

Dueling Adjustments

Many medical professionals agree that life's greatest stressors include the death of a spouse or loved one; divorce or separation; moving; major injury or illness; and, job loss. Others would add to the list marriage, imprisonment, buying or selling a home, and retirement.

Unfortunately, the trigger that compels some folks to consider settling in another country is often one of these life-altering experiences.

This brings to mind another important part of the planning process that I was glad I took the time to explore. If you're considering a major life change such as marriage or retirement (or if you have one thrust upon you such as the death of a spouse), is it wise to add another one of life's stressors to the mix at the same time?

In my case, retiring, selling my home and moving to Italy were three major stressors being experienced as one. Of course these were all by choice, but not lost on me was the fact that I would need to triple the careful thought, planning and preparation.

If you've lived with a spouse for a number of years and then suddenly you don't, it goes without saying that there will be adjustments. Managing the emotions alone will require daily drawing upon a reserve that you're not even sure you have. (As a young widow more than thirty years ago, I know whereof I speak.)

Maintaining a grueling work schedule, or even one that's not so grueling but just routine, and then waking up one day and not quite knowing what to do with yourself, is another adjustment that will require some attention, particularly if you haven't invested serious thought and planning into what your new lifestyle will look like.

The dangers that lie in not recognizing the gravity of these changes are many. Some people neglect their health, not giving proper attention to eating habits, weight, etc., perhaps overindulging in eating or drinking, or not maintaining a healthy exercise routine. For others, it's excessive spending, not having done the needed budgeting to accommodate a new, fixed income.

These life changes can make or break us, depending on how well we've planned for them. It is foolish to assume that we can manage even one of them without proper attention, let alone two or three. If one adjustment requires all of your attention, so be it. Perhaps it's best to handle that one before adding another.

While I've described some of the challenges of relocating to a new country, I have to repeat here that everyone's experience will be different. What was difficult for me may not be for someone else, and vice versa. Perhaps you've mastered the language and adapted to the culture, but you're having a hard time adjusting to that new spouse of yours. Or, maybe being a renter rather than a homeowner is working for you, but conditions on your new job are not.

A new expat life will always involve unknowns that cannot be planned for, but the same is true for other life changes. I tried to take all of this into account using only the "knowns" that I had to work with.

Not having staff meetings or deadlines, and not having to write about something that didn't even interest me, was a whole new world for me. While I already had a plan for health, self-care and spending, I hadn't given much thought to my daily schedule. (This is actually an important part of health and self-care, by the way.) I knew the things I would *need* to do, but not necessarily what I would *want* to do with the extra time I would have. Although I had worked remotely for many years in the States, even long before Covid, my time was still not my own. Now it would be.

All of this occurred to me almost as an afterthought during the planning process, but it was a huge eye-opener. Without even realizing it, I began to understand the important psychological aspects of simultaneous adjustments. Yes, my time was now my own, and I wasn't beholden to any rigid work schedules. I also didn't want to create new, rigid schedules for myself. To find that happy medium, I wanted to make the most of my new life of leisure without going overboard in either direction.

Fortunately, I had writing gigs of my own choosing, and I also wasn't one given to spending my days just lounging around. Having always been a fan of order and organization, it wasn't very difficult to design a regular schedule of language classes, writing, research, etc., along with leisurely walks, exploring, and other activities. I also delighted in the freedom of spontaneity—to change my mind and do something entirely unplanned with my day, or accept a last-minute invitation, etc.

Part of the freedom of retirement was choosing *not* to be a slug but to continue in a productive lifestyle of my own making. I even had designated "discovery days," when I might take a train ride to a town or village in search of the renowned ceramics or olive oils or open-air markets I'd read about. Sometimes I would discover nothing at all, or come away unimpressed with what I'd found, but having had an interesting, productive day nonetheless.

So, with the house sale and the physical move behind me, I was able to manage the remaining stressors of adjusting to retirement in addition to the expat adjustment of, well, being an expat. Again, I was thankful I'd recognized the need to consider the gravity of these changes *before* I made the move.

The unique challenges of managing multiple simultaneous life adjustments may just sound like more of that existential "know thyself" stuff, but they should be high on the list of priorities before undertaking the expat life.

We've talked about timing, and the wisdom of waiting or not waiting to make the big move. For some, it might be best to make these adjustments *before* moving to their new country. If managing stress is particularly difficult for you, why sabotage that vitally important self-care by inviting even more undue stress? At very least, recognize the challenges and be honest with yourself. It could make a world of difference in your ability to adjust to your new life.

* * *

Capisci?

A mong life's unchanging priorities, the importance of communication cannot be overstated. Even introverts like me recognize from a young age the need to understand what others are talking about and to get our own point across. When settling in another country, whether for business or any other reason, that priority is magnified one hundredfold.

Over the years, even when spending only a few weeks in a foreign country with an interpreter at hand, I always made the effort to at least learn some of the language's conversational basics. When staying long-term, I would even strive for some measure of fluency—partly out of respect and partly in an effort to survive and thrive. When I made the move to retirement in Italy, fluency was of course one of several goals. It leaped to the top of the list almost by accident.

As I've alluded to before, my whole expat move, from conception to planning to making it happen, was one big old lesson in accentuating the positive—finding the good stuff amongst the almost daily surprises and disappointments. I was able to put this into practice once again when I learned I would not be able to move into my apartment on the agreed date. I decided to rent an Airbnb in Firenze for a few weeks while I waited. This timing worked out perfectly in many ways, reminding me that everything happens for a reason.

First, there was the proximity to the government offices I needed to visit. There were also the much-needed language lessons.

During one of my pre-move recon trips, I'd spent a great deal of time on the train traveling from Florence to various villages to view potential abodes. During one particular week, in trying to keep appointments with realtors and property managers, the trains just would not cooperate. On one day alone, the train made an unscheduled stop in a small village for no apparent reason and passengers were urgently told to get off and board another train on a far-away track (which was actually headed in the opposite direction and would later circle back, thereby causing me to miss an appointment that day).

The amusing upside to this was that I was forced to figure out what the announcer was saying. It was either that or get hopelessly lost or left behind, or maybe just follow the other passengers to somewhere I didn't want to be.

While I'd been diligently studying Italian online on my own for a while, my language skills were still sorely lacking. I did okay in most brief conversations, but still had a hard time figuring out Italian speakers who seemed to be talking at breakneck speed. I've always contended that the only way to fully grasp another language is by immersion—trial by fire, if you will. I knew I couldn't begin to get comfortable with the Italian language until I was surrounded by it and forced to think on my feet, in Italian, in unexpected situations. My point was proven that day.

In Florence, as in Rome and Milan, there are many English speakers. But venturing out into most villages outside of major cities, this is not the case. I already knew I needed to be prepared to communicate solely in Italian, but I also knew I wasn't, so the extra time I had to spend in Florence before moving into my apartment was priceless.

I discovered that language schools abound in the center of Florence, from the Scuola Leonardo da Vinci to Parola, Europass and others, all with convenient choices of in-person, online, individual or group classes. Many of these are designed for students visiting from other countries and include accommodations. The major schools are all located within walking distance of the metropolitan center and, despite some Covid restrictions being partially lifted as of early 2022, group classes remained small and comfortable.

Several of these schools offer various levels of certifications, including CILS. The A2 level of CILS certification is recognized by the Ministry of Foreign Affairs as a valid certificate of competence in the Italian language (which is necessary for long-term residents to obtain the permanent EC

Residence Permit). And the exam for this certification is offered at the University of Siena as well as Parola and Scuola Leonardo da Vinci. Aspiring expats to any country should research the language proficiency requirements, and how and where to meet those requirements.

Language proficiency is not usually required or tested until you're applying for a permanent residence permit as opposed to a visa, and the permit stage typically comes after you've been in country for years. My need was not to meet any particular requirements. I just wanted to communicate comfortably.

I opted to begin my studies during my stay in Firenze with a combination of intensive group and personalized individual classes, both online. The classes may have been one of my richest early experiences in Italy. I already had a passable grasp of both Portuguese and Spanish, and knowledge of even one of the Romance languages is a built-in advantage when learning others. But, it didn't come as easily as I expected. With the language's many exceptions to so many rules, I realized I wouldn't be able to take this lightly. (After all the challenges and hard-fought victories, would the dreaded *verbi irregolari* and *verbi riflessivi* finally take me down?!)

Another advantage to taking language classes was connecting with my instructor, Marica. Patient and relatable, she not only listened to my stories and frustrations but, in a pretty crafty move, helped me share them in Italian. She also shared a few of her own challenges in a similar situation.

Recounting her experience of arriving in Paris a few years earlier for four years of study, and not speaking a word of French in the beginning, she helped to usher me out of self-pity mode and back to determination. (Apparently, the French were not as helpful and accommodating as the Italians.)

Although I didn't do in-person classes, most of my online classmates were also based right there in Florence. A few of us met for dinner or drinks several times over a four-week period, as socializing and communication outside of a classroom setting are crucial to a successful learning experience.

Of course, my immediate concern was communicating. But speaking of socializing, I also made it a practice to strike up conversations with strangers when sitting alone in a trattoria (thereby blowing my own mind, being the cranky old introvert that I am).

The *aperitivo* is an Italian pre-dinner tradition that is guaranteed to bring all stripes of executives, laborers, young, old, people from all walks of life out into the early evenings. I would talk to just about anyone within earshot. While there will always be folks who can't be bothered with being your impromptu language teacher, for the most part people were patient and willing to engage, many even anxious to help. I received suggestions on phone plans, shopping, the best train routes and schedules, finding the best off-the-beaten-path places to eat, and more.

Other new practices I adopted included responding and being willing to engage when others wanted to start conversations, and accepting invitations that the former me never would have considered.

While in Firenze, my Airbnb hosts asked if I wanted to join them for a drive to Siena. Mario and Anna spoke a little English, she more than he. It helped me tremendously to simply listen to Mario as he described the landscape and history of the villages we passed. Only rarely did I have to turn to Anna for clarification. As we drove, listening to Andrea Bocelli and chatting in Italian, it occurred to me that this was the most comfortable I'd felt with the language thus far.

Upon arriving in Siena, we climbed the steep cobblestone path up to the medieval Piazza de Campo. The huge piazza was filled with people, most just lying about on the ground, some strolling, children playing, etc. Some sort of bike race was about to take place, and a loudspeaker blared Rick James' *Superfreak*. (Which I found curious, but only for a minute. Just another Saturday morning in Siena, I guess.)

A major part of communication for me was being able to be comfortable. Getting past the tourist syndrome of finding everything odd was a big accomplishment. And, because I got to determine just how far out of my comfort zone I wanted to step on any given day, I was still able to enjoy the newness of the world around me while learning the language and the culture, all without stress or pressure.

After excursions like this, I would assess how much of the conversations I was picking up and retaining. There were always new words and phrases that I would practice using in sentences, even writing entire paragraphs and reading them back to myself. I was growing in fluency, almost in spite of myself.

Just as there are numerous regional dialects in the U.S. and other countries, the same is true in Italy. I realized another accomplishment the first time I recognized a Sicilian dialect among several speakers in a group conversation. These were the baby steps that I counted as huge triumphs, always worthy of a celebration.

Some of the most meaningful conversations I had in those days were just run-of-the-mill small talk, the kinds of chats that made me feel not so out of place. Even though I've never been a fan of small talk, I found that everyday banter was surprisingly helpful in establishing a brand new comfort zone.

And then there was Concetta.

While having a mid-morning cappuccino not far from my Airbnb, I noticed an elderly woman walk in and chat briefly with one of the servers. She placed her order and then came over and sat next to me. When I began chatting her up, she responded almost with relief, as if she was looking for someone to talk to. Maybe 75 or 80, Concetta had endless stories. She'd walked in haltingly with a cane, and proceeded to detail her physical ailments, complain about family members, and even how the quality of the establishment's cappuccino was not what it used to be. When she left, the server walked over and said *I see you met mia nonna* (my grandmother). I told him that, unfortunately, I only understood about half of what she had said. *Don't worry,* he assured me in Italian. *We all only understand half of what she says.*

Learning the ropes and getting great advice are important, but when someone can comfortably joke with you, it's a whole other level of communication. You may not yet be fluent, but you're well on your way.

* * *

Flying Solo. Or Not.

While it's crucial to consider adjusting to major changes in your personal life, you may have no such adjustments to worry about. Your goal may be to simply take your life as it is and move it to another place. Just geography, right?

As a single woman, I never took for granted the freedom of living life on my own terms—going out or staying in, eating the last piece of cake, spending or not, traveling or not, etc., etc. But, I don't think I really appreciated what a tremendous benefit this autonomy would be in my life as an expat.

When it came to the aforementioned adjusting and the all-too-frequent need to drop back and punt, I found that quick decisions in unexpected situations were often necessary. Those decisions might have been a lot more difficult had there been family interests to consider or a partner to consult.

I've met several expats who made their big move with young families in tow, and I'm still in awe of what they were able to accomplish while meeting the needs of each family member. From babies requiring a pediatrician to school-age children and all that that entailed, to two spouses whose careers both had to somehow fit into the big plan, and passports, visas and medical insurance for them all, I was exhausted just hearing the harrowing tales.

But, beyond the logistics of it all, there was the human element. Anyone who's ever lived life with a family knows it's never just about you, because every decision you make will affect others. And, even after you've taken the best interest of those others into account, they may not realize or appreciate it at the time. Certainly where children are concerned, their focus will not be on the logic or rationale of the matter, but on how *they* feel about the whole thing. (Because after all, kids only know how to focus on themselves. It's what they do.)

Because I was single for more than thirty years before moving to Italy, I already had the experience of making major life changes and adjustments on my own. Even with that arsenal of experience, there were all sorts of unfathomable challenges in my new expat life. While never having thought of myself as a selfish person, it was hard to imagine overcoming any of those challenges had I also had a family to worry about. I was pretty grateful to be flying solo.

Interesting to me were the parents who shared that, when making adjustments together with loved ones, they applied many of the same protocols as I did. In their planning and preparation, they knew they might be sacrificing many of the tried-and-true products they'd always used, as well as activities and hobbies they were used to, at least until they figured out where to find them in their new country. They took nothing for granted. And they were intentional about researching and finding those comforts that would simply make their family feel more at home, providing a bridge through their transition.

One single mom took language classes together with her children, ages eight and ten. Although not on the same level of proficiency, she provided them the comfort of the familiar, which was especially meaningful since she had home-schooled them back in the States during the pandemic. After four weeks of classes, and once they'd developed a good rapport with their instructor, the woman was able to separate into her own class. She told me that doing it that way made for a much more seamless transition and uninterrupted language studies.

Learning a new language is an area that will require different levels of adjustment within the family. Not only might each family member learn differently, but it is also well established that children pick up languages more quickly than adults. Here is where relocating with a family can have its advantages—you'll all be there to help one another, and even find the fun in the process, if you so choose.

Of course, families and singles each have their own unique challenges. But, finding or creating familiar comforts is important in both cases, not necessarily to remind us of home, but to feed that longing in each one of us for whatever it is that just makes us *feel* comfortable in a new place. Although some recreational pursuits may be different, perhaps there's a hobby or activity that's just as accessible in the new country as it was in the old.

Another family I knew were avid bikers. When they moved to Tuscany, they continued biking together every weekend. When I saw the three kids and their parents on their bikes one Saturday morning, chattering and giggling, they looked as comfortable and relaxed as any family pursuing their favorite pastime in their hometown.

As mentioned, one of the things I had to be intentional about was engaging with strangers in an effort to become more conversational in Italian. This was out of my comfort zone, but especially as a single, it was necessary in order to reach that language goal. And because of this practice, I was able to make a few good friends early on.

In addition to my gracious landlords, who held my hand through some of the most confusing and overwhelming bureaucracy, I had the great pleasure of connecting with another special couple. Mimmo and Elisabetta are owners of what became one of my favorite Firenze haunts, Ristorante da Mimmo. They spoke no English at all, but through their multilingual hostess Rahma, they were happy to engage. They even threw me an impromptu birthday celebration one evening after I'd enjoyed one of Mimmo's amazing meals. And, when Rahma returned to her home country of Tunisia to give birth, Mimmo, Elisabetta and I continued to amuse ourselves with our clumsy attempts to communicate.

I was grateful for these connections, and they did indeed enhance my language skills. But, they also provided a home-like sense of comfort. Whether single or a family member, introvert or social butterfly, this matters.

Just like those families I'd met, I also knew it was important to find familiar activities as a single, having nothing at all to do with checklists or goals like mastering the language. I found this bridge from my old life to the new, in a new church and an Argentine tango class.

For me, my church back home was not only a place of spiritual fulfillment but provided a social outlet with likeminded fellow parishioners. In visiting similar churches around the world over the years, I knew we spoke a universal language. I was sure that attending a new church in Firenze would be a joy rather than a challenge, and I was right. After visiting a few different churches, both of the denomination I'd practiced in the past and of other denominations for curiosity's sake, I chose a small church that was comfortable and welcoming. Although I found English-speaking churches in the region, I was deliberate about my choice of an Italian-speaking one. And, as an added bonus, listening to the pastor each week and striking up conversations with those around me became part of my language studies.

My second bridge to my past life was Argentine tango. I had practiced and danced the tango for several years back in the States—not necessarily well, but it was one of those pursuits that fed my soul at its deepest levels. It's a closely knit worldwide community, and I had already come across classes and gatherings at events known as *milongas* in other countries. Although I usually found expert dancers at these milongas while I could do little more than ogle, there was still something warm and familiar in their environment.

It took no time at all to find a weekly milonga in Firenze, and a small class in Lucca Province. Since talking on the dance floor is against etiquette, it didn't matter that I didn't yet have the strongest grasp of Italian. And, just like the pastor at church, the dance instructors spoke a universal language. I felt instantly welcome. It provided a bit of an escape, and I've since learned of other groups throughout the Toscana region.

As trivial as it may sound, finding those tango gatherings was critical to my mental and emotional health as a new expat, just as those four weeks of studying Italian with their mom were to her children. As much as we all want to experience the new stuff and that whole "other" life we may have looked forward to, never underestimate the importance of the familiar. Those activities and environments that have always provided comfort, or just an escape from the demands of life, are still there for us.

You probably know what I'm going to say here, but it bears repeating—you've got to know yourself! And, if you're part of a family, you must know and understand the needs of each family member. Don't take for granted the everyday activities and experiences that you really don't want to let go of. It's okay to hang on to them.

Whether you're a family or flying solo, take care to figure familiar hobbies, habits and recreational pursuits into the equation, and make them a part of your planning process. This may make all the difference to the big picture.

* * *

Entertainment Value

As discussed, we probably all have certain recreational escapes that we want to keep in our new country. For some of us, these include certain forms of entertainment that are so integral to our lives that we wouldn't dream of giving them up.

Besides dark chocolate and great wine, most of my weaknesses seem to fall into an artistic category, including reading and the theater. There are those forms of entertainment that include the 25th anniversary stage production of *Les Miserables,* with Alfie Boe and Norm Lewis as rivals Valjean and Javert; anything in Yo Yo Ma's repertoire; and, yet another reading of *The Agony and the Ecstasy.*

When indulging in these delights, I simply cannot be interrupted or distracted—they have my undivided, rapt, spellbound attention. They are some of my most meaningful and enjoyable means of entertainment. And they were included in the small collection of books, DVDs, and playlists that accompanied me to Italy.

Some things just become a part of us. No matter what stage of my career or personal life, no matter how stressful a particular workday, my favorite literature, music, movies and stage productions always provided that much-needed escape. I couldn't imagine a world where I wouldn't be able to pick up a volume of Gabriel Garcia Marquez or pop in an old Bette Davis or Sidney Poitier movie at will. So, these collections figured prominently into my detailed packing plan.

There are a couple of ways to view an escape. One is escaping *from* the thing or place from which you desperately want to be extricated; the other is escaping *to* a place where you find delight, whimsy, peace, etc., even if the place you're escaping from is just fine. (Most folks would probably place their island vacations in that latter category, but I wonder if perhaps those escapes might actually be *from* their crazy, suffocating workplaces. Just sayin'.)

In any case, I find neither of these escapes to be a bad thing. In fact, I would think they're probably both necessary to our overall health and wholeness.

I allowed myself to escape *from* the craziness and confusion of becoming a new expat, and also to escape *to* that place of delight, even if I was already having a great day—in fact, that latter escape might just make a great day perfect.

While I've emphasized the importance of maintaining hobbies and familiar habits and comforts, entertainment was something else entirely in my new expat life. I wanted to immerse myself in Italian culture and entertainment, not only to aid in my language command, but to explore new indulgences that I might find as engrossing as those I already treasured. (I also wanted to be careful to steer clear of the mindlessness we find on television and on the internet, no matter where we live.)

Italian entertainment ended up serving several equally important purposes for me, and still does. I would sometimes watch the crime channel that aired dubbed versions of old *Columbo* or *Law and Order* episodes, two past addictions of mine in the States. Because I knew the storylines of just about every episode by heart, hearing the dialogue in Italian became a fun part of learning the language, without any of the frustrations of studying. There were also Italian true crime programs that I had to work hard to understand. But, being a true crime addict, even this didn't seem at all like work to me.

I also watched Italian news channels, opera channels, cooking shows, and even an occasional talk show. While I may have understood little of what was being said in the beginning, I did know what was going on. Eventually, the words came. Dialogues began to make sense. I could laugh at a joke, disagree with an opinion, or become incensed at a current event.

Then there was the Airbnb in Firenze that contained a library of Italian classics as well as a complete set of encyclopedias. It was like striking gold. I was hooked. I would frequently pick up a volume in the evening and curl up with a glass of wine while perusing the entries on geographical sites or historical figures.

If these typical evenings at home sound all too familiar, that's my point. And that was precisely my goal.

In an age of social media-induced overstimulation, it goes unsaid that there must be limits to our entertainment escapes. And, it's especially tempting in unfamiliar surroundings to indulge in the aforesaid mindlessness.

The effects of entertainment, particularly on young people and families, have been researched going all the way back to Sesame Street more than fifty years ago.

In a 2019 New York Times essay, Brookings Institute Fellow Jonathan Rothwell wrote,

> *Other than sleeping and working, Americans are more likely to watch television than engage in any other activity.*
>
> *A wave of new social science research shows that the quality of shows can influence us in important ways, shaping our thinking and political preferences, even affecting our cognitive ability.*
>
> *In this so-called golden age of television, some critics have pointed out that the best of the form is equivalent to the most enriching novels. And high-quality programming for children can be educational. But the latest evidence also suggests there can be negative consequences to our abundant watching, particularly when the shows are mostly entertainment.*

> *The harm seems to come not so much from the content itself but from the fact that it replaces more enlightening ways of spending time.*

Good point. Particularly because our society now counts social media as entertainment as well as an information source, we might first assess the content we choose to consume. Moreover, if our expat quest is all about continued growth, then we would do well not to stray too far from those objectives. Period. This, of course, is the case no matter where we may choose to live. If we're careful to maintain this balance, entertainment can be an important part of a less stressful expat life.

The value of our various forms of entertainment may be incalculable. For me, it was priceless in acclimating to a new land. Both the English language entertainment that I brought with me, and the new Italian entertainment that I adopted and adapted to, were essential to finding my comfort zone. In moderation, they both continue to provide those much-needed *from* and *to* escapes.

Of course, my existing collection of literature and DVDs will always be with me, whether here in Italy or anywhere else. They are a part of me. But, as an added bonus, some of my new Italian favorites came to occupy a new place among those old treasures. When I ordered my first Italian DVD, the classic 1945 film *Roma Citta Aperta*, I knew it had joined the ranks of those inescapable weaknesses. As for television, no real weaknesses yet, but there are a couple of story lines that are definitely coming close.

One last word about entertainment in your new country. FCC regulations we all take for granted may be very different under foreign regulatory bodies. Content that is the norm in one region may be considered soft porn in another. Particularly if there are children in your household, this is an area where you don't want to be caught unawares!

* * *

Go Time

The time had come. I had come to understand and learned to embrace the psychology of it all; I'd done as much advance research and planning as humanly possible; I'd found an apartment and signed a lease agreement; and, I had said my good-byes.

I remember the very last day before leaving the country. I was at an airport hotel getting ready for my early morning flight. I'd had my Covid test that morning and just received the negative results by email, and that had been the final step. (I'd been holding my breath for several hours waiting for those make-or-break results.)

And now, everything was done, a reality that had only really hit me when I realized I had no keys. None. After the sale of my home and car, I had, perhaps for the first time in sixty years, no keys. I talked to my son on the phone that morning. *So, how do you feel, Mom?*, he asked. The first word that came out of my mouth was surprising even to me. *Unencumbered,* I said.

One of my choices from the beginning was to sell my U.S. home rather than rent it out or keep it for whatever reason. I'd been a landlord before and didn't ever want to do that again. Nor did I want to undertake the responsibility of being an Airbnb host or keeping and maintaining the home for that mysterious, unknown what-if-one-day-maybe event. Thankfully, it was a seller's market, with the prospect of excellent profits. Sure, selling a home is still nerve-wracking in any market, but the timing in my case couldn't have been more perfect. And there was another consideration.

Whether flipping, downsizing, or relocating for work, it always feels good to complete the sale of a house—but never so good as when you just don't want a house. I had spent the last couple of years rediscovering the minimalist lifestyle that I lived years earlier in Angola. Letting go of stuff and, more importantly, giving stuff away, were liberating—and conducive to good staging as it turned out, making the house more sellable than ever.

This is another one of those areas that may require some adjustment for the aspiring or new expat. Are you ready to get by without the stuff you're used to? Perhaps you're not a fan of minimalism, and not ready to let go of many of your belongings. Some folks choose not only to keep their stuff, but to ship it across the ocean— furniture, cars, and more. If you're one of those people, please think of the expense, the logistics, and the legalities involved. As for your car, how prepared are you to acquire your new driver's license and begin driving unfamiliar terrain? You may want to get the lay of the land before shipping your vehicle.

Purging was interesting, even cathartic, but so was the packing process. Once again, it comes down to what you really need and what you really want, and eliminating the extraneous.

When it came to packing, the list that helped determine what I would bring with me endured countless modifications. Since the flat I rented in Lucca Province was fully furnished and equipped, my grand plan was to pack two huge suitcases—one with clothes, shoes, and small incidentals, and one with paperwork, photos, the aforementioned books and DVDs, plus my weird old giant computer briefcase that I'd had since my days as a newspaperwoman. Other near-and-dear items would be left in storage with family, to be retrieved later.

After reading an account written by a fairly new expat of her packing regrets, I had to rethink things a bit. She was surprised to discover some of the things she wished she'd stocked up on were the brands of toiletries, cosmetics and OTC meds she was used to. Because many of her usual brands were not available in her new home country, she advised bringing a supply that would last through the trial-and-error process of finding comparable products. Point taken.

Researching whether Amazon delivers to your new location is one way of knowing beforehand what products will be available, until you're on the ground and can start shopping locally.

Once I was moved in and beginning to get settled in my new digs, of course there were all sorts of things I wished I had brought, and others I wished I hadn't. My landlords, who have since become good friends, were instrumental in directing me where to shop for various items, and probably saving me lots of euros.

This settling-in period, by the way, should be as stress-free as possible. I made lots of mental notes of things I needed, but I was in no hurry to rush out and stock my cupboards right away. There was plenty else to do, and so much I had already accomplished, that I felt I deserved a break. As soon as I was able, I was pretty intentional about taking time to put my feet up and absorb the beauty of my surroundings.

After working out WiFi and utility matters with my landlords and taking care of a few other administrative requirements, this leisurely unpacking process was one of the things that made me know I was home. It was then that I was able to take a breath and focus a bit on what I was leaving behind.

When embarking on your own pursuit of an expat life, this is an important step. Take a good long look back, and be thorough, leaving nothing undone. Embrace what matters, whether it's experiences or relationships. If closure is needed, get closure.

For folks who've made their expat decision, and even their move, without that oh-so-important introspection discussed earlier, the need to do this is not going away. So, here are a few tips: Recognize what and whom you'll miss, and how to stay connected. (Personally, before I even arrived in Italy I had planned my first trip back to the States for my granddaughter's graduation, as well as weekly virtual coffees with a couple of good friends.)

Make a point of sticking to any planned calls or get-togethers. We always say *Let's keep in touch* when we part ways, but the lesson here would be not to say it unless you mean it. And then, do it. Even if you've just promised to shoot a text or email update to certain folks every couple of weeks or so, you'll be surprised at how good it will feel to keep that promise.

During a WhatsApp chat with an old friend, she asked if I had any new adventures to report. I wanted to remind her that I'm not here in search of adventure. I'm a retiree just looking for a little quiet. But, it turns out that every day is indeed an adventure, and I imagine it always will be. In this new chapter of life, in this new country, I have no doubt that every day will be a day of discovery. After all, it took more than sixty years to see and fully appreciate my home country.

Allowing yourself to miss what you loved about home may be part of what will help you to love your new country. Giving yourself permission to reminisce and get a little nostalgic now and then is a good thing. It speaks to wholeness—bringing together those parts and pieces to make a seamless transition from the old life to the new.

This transition became important to me. Unbeknownst to me, I had built a solid bridge, so that I didn't have to let go of anything behind me but I still got to embrace everything up ahead. As a matter of fact, in retrospect, I don't think either one of those is even possible without the other. (So, if you're all about burning bridges, the expat life may not be the right path toward that goal.)

After the looking back comes the looking forward. I'm still finding it hard to believe, but reality is slowly sinking in. I've embraced my huge, unimaginable aspirations and finally joined the ever-growing ranks of expats who've embraced theirs. And I look forward to each day, partly because I know each day will bring surprises—some good, some not so much, but as I said earlier, it's never dull!

For those still wondering if you can do this, the answer is a resounding *YES.* You can figure out the visas, the rules and legalities, the employment and tax and insurance and language issues. So, knowing that you can, the only remaining question is if you *will*.

Consider again the reasons why so many people never end up making their big move, or why they hesitate. Perhaps it's time to start examining those reasons for yourself, one by one. Perhaps it's your go time.

Life is short. Find the place that feeds your soul—and live it there.

* * *

Exploration

I would imagine one of the common denominators among expats is curiosity about their new home. Not just what to see and what to do, but how it became the country it is today. For many of us, what we learned in school about our own country was just a small fraction of the big picture. And, in our new country, we have even less to start with.

Exploration becomes a passion, especially for those who may not have spent much time there before relocating. Workers occupy their "discovery" evenings and weekends getting out and about, while retirees may take advantage of the weekdays' quieter, less crowded streets and shops. High on many lists is getting away from the cities and touristy areas, to investigate lesser-known towns and hamlets. During my first few months here in Italy, I did just that.

Exploring the towns and villages throughout Tuscany quickly became an obsession for me. I thought I had learned so much from past visits and research, but when you're talking about a region that is thousands of years old, there's just no end to what one can learn. Being a bit of a history geek, there were certain things that were most appealing to me. The bygone events, bizarre facts and tidbits of unexpected information had me captivated. But, I was careful to take my time to absorb things, rather than just doing the tourist tromp through each region and not really coming away any richer or more knowledgeable about my new country.

On one leisurely drive with a couple of new friends, we stopped to spend some time in the village of San Gimignano. Situated in Siena Province about an hour south of Florence, this village of fewer than 10,000 people holds some serious intrigue, especially for history buffs.

Dating all the way back to the Etruscans, around 63 B.C., San Gimignano was officially founded in the 900s. Two of its claims to fame are its saffron cultivation dating back to 1200, and its Vernaccia wine. But, its towers and walls were the clinchers. Of its original 72 towers, 14 are still standing, and they cut an impressive figure when viewing the landscape as you approach the hilltop city.

San Gimignano's past is fascinating to me for the same reason as Lucca's—those walls surrounding the city. These are two of just a few medieval cities whose walls are still standing, probably the most famous being Siena. There is just something about medieval walls still standing after two thousand years—the defense and protection they provided for a city way back then, and the escape they provide for us today. Strolling along Lucca's walls on a sunny afternoon is now one of my favorite things to do for a break from studying or writing.

Another interesting (and very creepy) discovery in San Gimignano was its torture museum. At first, I wasn't sure it was really a thing. Not only was it real, but sure enough, I learned there are torture museums in five of Tuscany's medieval towns and villages. They bill themselves as torture and death penalty museums, but make it clear that they are not celebrating torture; instead, they are "an exhibition in which the horror aroused in the spectators at the vision of the instruments allows us to make them our allies in the fight against torture." Okay, fine, but I still wasn't about to go in there. Unlike the museums that evoke reflection and mourning in tribute to Holocaust or lynching victims, for me this stuff was just unviewable.

The torture museum being situated right next door to a Leonardo da Vinci museum made for quite a contrast. (Let's see…art and science or sadistic brutality? Hmmm.) It was also interesting to learn the important political roles that the likes of Dante and Macchiavelli played in the city's history. For such a small, rural commune that many may never have heard of, when visiting San Gimignano it's amazing that a couple of hours isn't even a fraction of the time you'll need to absorb it all.

The historical richness I'm gaining here in Italy cannot be overstated. Because of the advanced age and fascinating origins of so many cities in this country and throughout Europe, I would hope that all expats would be equally excited to learn more through exploration. I mean, torture museums? Really? You can't make this stuff up.

Besides what can be learned from just exploring the countryside, museums and ancient architecture and monuments of course hold a wealth of historical information. My fascination with museums has taken me from the Hermitage to the Louvre, the Picasso and Gaudi, to the Met and the Uffizi. But, taking my granddaughter to visit the Smithsonian soon after the opening of the National Museum of African American History and Culture was the joy of a lifetime. Touring the Washington, D.C. monuments and being able to take her aside at each stop and tell her "the rest of the story" brought tremendous gratification.

When park ranger Betty Reid Soskin retired from the National Park Service at the age of one hundred in early 2022, I learned of the compelling historical perspective she had brought to her work. While leading public programs at the Rosie the Riveter/WWII Home Front National Historical Park in Richmond, CA, Soskin shared stories of her own experiences as a woman of color on the home front during World War II. If not for her service, these accounts would never have been known from our history books alone.

Soskin said, *What gets remembered is a function of who's in the room doing the remembering.*

There is always more to the story. And, in any country, those who are best equipped to share such historical wealth are usually the elderly. These are the folks with first-hand accounts, or history passed down through generations. They're often celebrated and their stories shared in museum exhibits. But, as a new expat, I've also been enjoying meeting seniors and hearing first-hand their take on the people and events of the past. While some societies may not value the wisdom of age, in my experience most European countries do.

Even if art and history are not your thing, consider the obligatory aspect of learning through exploration. As a new resident of Italy, I felt responsible to know a little about the place. Also consider the mandatory aspects. If you plan to become a permanent resident in any country, there are a bunch of facts that you'll have to know. And there will be a test.

* * *

Seasons

I just heard the news that the U.S. has passed a measure abolishing the bi-annual practice of changing clocks, and adopting permanent daylight saving time. (I couldn't help but notice that they waited until after I left.)

As much as I love daylight and always looked forward to springing forward, I also hated the early morning commutes in the dark. For me, it's a six-of-one type of deal. But, my hope is that the rest of the world that is currently changing its clocks will follow the U.S.'s lead. Personally, I've always thought the whole clock-changing process is part of what makes us all crazy.

Growing up in New Jersey, before global warming began to have the impact we're seeing today, the winters were bitter cold. I hated them. The long walks to and from school with the snow, ice and bone-chilling temperatures were unbearable. I hated the darkness and endless overcast skies. As a child, even the anticipation of the holidays didn't lessen my loathing of the winter season. I would spend months just looking forward to the spring cherry blossoms.

My hands-down season of choice has always been spring. Even without turning our clocks forward, having to wait a bit for evening daylight would not have diminished the glory of the season for me. No matter the country or climate in which I found myself, I always relished the time of year for budding and blooming, and yes, daylight. So, my anticipation of springtime in Italy was through the roof.

If you're anything like me, once you're on the ground in your new country there will be countless unexpected observations. One of these for me was the equal importance of all four seasons, on a number of different levels.

While the region of Tuscany has been romanticized in novels and movies, and I already knew that its beauty is second to none, I couldn't wait to actually live out a Tuscan spring. I was not disappointed. With the world around me in bloom and folks strolling the piazzas late into the evenings, my first spring in Italy was a daily sight to behold. But, beyond the sights and sounds, there was so much more to learn. I was pleased to find that many of these lessons centered around food.

Of course the freshest foods anywhere are based on seasonal and regional availability, but eating seasonally is more of a mainstay of the Italian way of life. Especially in smaller towns and villages, locals shop several times a week, sometimes daily, rather than shopping in bulk and storing foods for days or weeks. Cooking with the freshest foods seems to be much more common, and there are stringent regulations barring certain methods of preserving foods.

Like everyone else who's visited Italy, I've always raved about the cuisine, but maybe because of our comfort zone of preserving and storing foods for long periods, this focus on fresh foods may not have even occurred to many of us.

Given the freshness of ingredients, the celebrated delectability of Italian cuisine was kind of obvious. And it's certainly not news to those who pay attention to such things, whether at home or anywhere in the world. I just wasn't one of those people. I'd always simply picked out what looked freshest at the supermarket, or what sounded tastiest on the menu. But in Italy, I started paying attention to things like growing seasons. Once I learned the best times to buy certain foods, it all made a lot more sense. The asparagus, zucchini, artichokes and strawberries that saw me through my first spring were perfection, and made my mouth water for summer's melons, peppers and tomatoes.

Of course, foods are still preserved here like anywhere, and delicious meals are served year-round (so don't be discouraged if you're visiting in the off-season). But processed foods are much less abundant, and the integral role that fresh foods play in welcoming Italian seasons taught me a great deal about the culture itself.

Italy's festivals and many other cultural traditions are also largely seasonal, not the least of which are the Christmas Markets. While the mid-to late-summer tourist season is known for certain traditions, the discovery of lesser-known customs and celebrations was more rewarding for me. As not only a lover of springtime but also someone who usually dreads winter, I was pretty surprised at how much I found myself looking forward to the cold weather season in Italy. I was excited about experiencing the culture of winter, rather than the weather.

During one of my reconnaissance trips in the fall of 2021, the winds were chilly and I thought the rain would never stop. There were a few Christmas decorations, but the official Christmas Markets had not yet opened. Already exasperated with the work of checking boxes on my agenda, I also found myself feeling pretty grumpy on most days. I was glad I was here on a fact-finding mission rather than a vacation getaway, or I would have been sorely disappointed. I was also glad I wasn't basing my decision to move here on the winter climate.

In the U.S., I lived in Louisiana for several years because of a career opportunity. It would never have been my preference to live in what I considered an oppressively humid climate. Once I was able to work remotely, I chose the dry, desert air of New Mexico to call home.

Such options are common in larger countries with more diverse climates. Many American northerners, for example, will summer in Florida or in the southwest. But, in a smaller country like Italy, the weather is fairly uniform throughout (although somewhat cooler in the north toward the

Alps, and hotter and more humid in the south). Many retirees don't have the luxury of a summer home in another country or region in any case, and must stay put year-round wherever they decide to call home. Here again is where balance comes in.

Although the climate was my primary reason for moving to New Mexico, it hadn't really occurred to me how much I would also love getting to know its culture and seasonal traditions. I embraced the Native American history and art, the springtime Gathering of Nations, the Christmas luminarias, the biscochitos and green chiles. The climate took a back seat to the richness of the region, and it's that richness that I still miss.

I would guess there is a large majority of folks who prefer the spring season as I do, probably for many of the same reasons. The mental health benefits of springtime are well-settled in psychology circles. The season just looks better and feels better. But, there are also those who look forward to their annual summer break from school, or football or ski season, or the holidays, above all else. As an avid tennis fan who also enjoys hitting a few balls when I can, I have yet another reason to prefer warmer weather. But now, as a new resident of a land where everything is a cultural learning experience, I'm much more motivated to embrace the seasons year-round.

As discussed earlier, bringing the comforts of home with us to our new country is a great idea, including our preferences for particular seasons and their respective activities. But, once I allowed myself to look beyond my own preconceived notions and expectations, what a joy I have found in looking at seasons differently here in Italia.

* * *

Where Faith Comes In

Fullness, gratification, the feeding of my soul—these can all be summed up pretty easily for me, because they're all a by-product of my Christian faith.

Yes, there are existential and circumstantial outcomes in life which are an important part of the whole. But for me, faith is the umbrella, the key, the vessel that contains it all. So, whatever your belief system may be, allow me to posit a few thoughts on the role it plays in this crazy—I mean, wonderful—life decision you've made.

A word about spirituality— it's not a one-time experience to cross off your checklist, or an *Eat, Pray, Love* sort of infusion of religiosity or rung on the ladder of life. Just as dieting is a bad idea as opposed to a lifestyle of healthy eating, spirituality is not a temporary fix to get you to one particular goal. It's about making a choice already, which can only come with truly knowing yourself. (Otherwise, those choices are not yours. They're subject to the direction of the winds, or whatever belief system may be society's flavor of the month.)

While Catholicism is the predominant religion practiced here in Italy, and I am a Protestant, there is something comforting to me about Italians' general reverence for their faith. I've found this veneration just about everywhere here, among both ardent believers and those who are not. It is an element of the culture that I admire.

Here again is where we would do well to know from whence we derive our comfort and well-being. If it is in our faith, then what is it about that faith that gives us our peace?

If you're not a person of faith, just being able to figure out the answers to those questions could make a tremendous difference in your process of finding your place and settling there. But, if you are a person of faith, you would do well to have your faith walk figured out before embarking on your expat life. Otherwise, you'll be back to navigating those dueling adjustments. In other words, you'll be a hot mess, having created all sorts of undue angst.

Obviously, not everyone's faith is rooted in Christianity. But, for those making the life-changing decision to relocate to another country, I can't imagine how this can be accomplished without seeking spiritual wisdom and guidance according to your own beliefs. Trust me—it would behoove you to decide for once and for all who you're going to be. Then go and be that, building on that foundation and continuing to be who you are, whether in your home country or somewhere else.

Even if you're already well-grounded in your chosen belief system, there is still going to be that whole daily getting up in the morning and walking it out challenge.

I have fought the good fight, I have finished the race, I have kept the faith.
                                    2 Timothy 4:7

Any race, any competition, any journey, will involve a fight of some sort, on some level. For many, life itself is a perpetual battle. So, in order to finish the race and keep the faith, you have to fight the good fight. (Well, hopefully a good one. There are lots of folks out there fighting a whole other kind of fight. That's another choice we get to make.) But what does that even mean? If we're so busy putting out fires and trying to stay on our feet in the ring, how can we even define, let alone take control of this battle?

The "good fight" Scripture has been bandied about and employed in different contexts since forever. But I took it quite seriously. I had always hoped I would one day be able to honestly utter those words, even though I knew my inner selfishness, snarkiness, and general disdain for (some) other human beings might hinder that goal.

During times of introspection on my journey to Italy, I concluded that fighting the good fight at this stage of life would mean a steadfast, unwavering determination to simply "finish well." Okay, maybe not simple, but it was one singular, overarching goal.

In exploring what finishing well would look like for me, I discovered that its components were manifold. Fulfilling the purpose for which God put me on this earth to begin with; feeding my own soul; finding the good stuff (i.e., accentuating the positive and not dwelling on the junk—you know, eating the meat and spitting out the bones).

The time of solitude before I met my neighbors and made a couple of friends, the time of not knowing what I was doing, getting lost while bumming around exploring, experiencing those constant setbacks and disappointments, fighting trepidation all along the way, and coming to terms with a vulnerability I had always battled against, was a time of deepening my faith. I reached an understanding that a little vulnerability was okay; that the setbacks and disappointments made me stronger; that the time would come (and indeed it did) when my new home would finally feel like home.

Had faith not been there from the beginning, each and every one of those battles would likely have been lost. And, without having made this unthinkable transition to Italy, the race as it was designed for me would certainly not be complete.

* * *

Happy

Many people have asked me if I would ever go back to the United States to live. Of course, there is no way to know the answer to that question. I love my home country and there are certainly many things and people that I miss. Coming to terms with some of the truths that compelled me to leave was a sad exercise. Not believing things would change for the better during my lifetime was even harder to face. But, deciding that I deserved better, and setting out to find that better, was one of the most affirming choices I've made. And the process, although challenging and frustrating, was a happy time.

We've talked about gratification and fulfillment, but what about happiness? Its relevance to this discussion depends a lot on your definition. I've always seen happiness as circumstantial, as opposed to *joy*, which I see as a deep, abiding condition and not dependent on where you live or the ups and downs of everyday life.

In an earlier chapter I alluded to the small parts that comprise the whole of life. I'm reminded of a scene at the end of the enduring movie, *The Pursuit of Happyness* (yes, that's how they spelled it). The biopic about stockbroker Chris Gardner depicted his life of parts and pieces fraught with trials, setbacks, hope, and more setbacks. After striving relentlessly for a particular career goal, one that would set the stage for ultimate lifelong success, the day came when he was rewarded with his first huge job offer. The character's final line in the movie was, *This part of my life...this little part...is called happiness.*

That scene spoke volumes. In an interview, Gardner said he knew that getting the job would not guarantee lifetime happiness, but he allowed himself to savor the happiness of that moment.

Social scientist and columnist Arthur Brooks has written extensively on the topic of happiness. At the height of the pandemic, Brooks also addressed the increasingly popular idea of relocating. In a 2021 installment of his column in *The Atlantic*, he wrote:

> *... feeling out of place, and as though where you live is not truly your home. That might be especially true today, when so many people have been involuntarily displaced by the pandemic or are stuck in living situations not of their own choosing. But this upheaval could also provide an opportunity. As the economy changes, and quarantine has revealed that many jobs can be performed remotely, you*

might find yourself with more geographic flexibility than you have had in a long time. If you're uncomfortable with the status quo, this time when life has been paused might be just the impetus you need to make you consider a change of place. This year could be the chance for you to move to the place where your heart resides.

In his podcast, *The Art of Happiness,* Brooks contends that happiness is 50% genetic, 25% circumstantial, and 25% in your control. Our goal should be to focus on that last 25% and *build a portfolio of happiness habits to live a life that is balanced and full of meaning, and that serves your values.*

It sounds like a lot to unpack, but according to Brooks, this roadmap to living a happier life is based on scientific research with practical applications to everyday life. For us laypeople, the concept just makes good practical sense.

I believe the building of your portfolio of happiness habits is an exercise in keeping with my emphasis on research and knowing oneself. Honestly assessing what it would take to make me happy and figuring out where in the world I would find those ingredients were key in reaching the decision to live in Italy.

Once again, we're not talking about a condition of joy. This is about circumstantial things and things that you can control.

In March of 2022, for the tenth consecutive year, the United Nations Sustainable Development

Solutions Network (SDSN) issued its World Happiness Report. Drawing on data gathered from 150 nations, the report attempts to determine the happiest and least happy countries, and discusses the criteria for increased happiness. One of those criteria is benevolence, which SDSN reports has increased globally, ostensibly as a result of the pandemic. Activities such as donating to charity, helping strangers and volunteering increased by 25% in 2021 compared to pre-pandemic levels.

Other factors considered in this annual assessment include healthy life expectancy, GDP per capita, social support, low corruption, and personal freedom—all pretty obvious happiness ingredients. Based on such factors, Nordic countries have been deemed the happiest on earth for several consecutive years, with Finland, Denmark, Iceland, Switzerland and the Netherlands ranking as 2021's top five.

Again, these factors are the obvious things that we would all want in our chosen home country—but, other than benevolence, they are largely out of our personal control.

When choosing my new home country, I not only focused on the big things, but the small everyday things that I enjoy personally. I wanted to be able to practice the carefree, relaxing habits that made me happy, such as a quiet afternoon train ride through the rolling hills of Tuscany; a stroll through a vineyard or olive grove; reading on a bench in a medieval piazza filled with people lying about and minding their own business; a daily cappuccino in a quiet pasticceria (i.e., an anti-Starbucks); or, sitting with my laptop on my terrace overlooking a picturesque landscape (my new definition of work).

Visiting bookstores also ranks among these delights. I've found new and used volumes, sometimes in obscure stores in remote corners of the tiniest villages. One of the reasons for my newfound love of train travel is the amazing bookstore inexplicably located in the Santa Maria Novella station in Firenze's metropolitan center.

These were the things that fed my soul and that I could do comfortably, whenever I wanted, without any particular effort or cost. I had no interest in contrived experiences that required downloading yet another app, or had to be planned and paid for, or the latest trendy, hipster activities (Ax throwing? Really??), or conditions and opportunities that require years of begging the government to legislate.

While I've talked about the need for the occasional escape via things like entertainment, happiness can also be associated with the quiet, the meditative, the relaxing, and what I call the "do-nothing" types of fun. Even for those landing in a new country for work, or the driven types who have a need to be on the go nonstop, trust me, those do-nothing times are important. Any wannabe expat, not just retirees, might want to think not only of all that must or can be done, but what can be *eliminated* from our daily routine. And the non-activity that can be added.

In my book, *An Epic Odyssey of Madness and Mayhem,* I discussed the need for a little whimsy in our lives, suggesting that one ingredient in happiness might just be allowing ourselves to frolic a bit:

> ... *by whimsy, I'm thinking of a whole different kind of escape. Like the young man who posted footage of himself skipping through a field with reckless abandon, leaping and clicking his heels. The post included an unexpected explanation: "I frolicked for the first time today, bruh. Y'all ever frolic before? How come no one ever told me about this?"*

Once his tweet went viral, he followed up with words of wisdom: "If you're having a bad day, just frolic. I promise, you'll feel better."

So, if you're wondering if you can find happiness in a new country, you might just ask yourself: Will there be whimsy? Will there be time to frolic?

Not being a social scientist, I'll just venture a guess here. A key element of happiness may just be living in the moment. Notwithstanding all the anal-retentive planning and preparation it took to get here, these days I find myself smelling and appreciating a lot more roses.

Whether or not I'll live in the U.S. again remains to be seen, but one of the great things about choosing happiness from day to day is having no pressure to make that long-term decision. Should circumstances change, either here or there, who knows? In the meantime, I'll be on the terrace.

* * *

www.ingramcontent.com/pod-product-compliance
Lightning Source LLC
La Vergne TN
LVHW090046090426
835511LV00031B/325